The Woman's Book of Revenge

Christine Gallagher was born in England. She has worked as a public relations writer, written, produced and directed television programmes and is a freelance journalist. She has won several awards for her television work and her first screenplay, *Halfway There*, won Steven Spielberg's Diane Thomas Screenwriting Award. She is married with two sons and lives in L.A.

THE
Woman's Book
OF
Revenge

GETTING EVEN WHEN 'MR RIGHT' TURNS OUT TO BE ALL WRONG

Christine Gallagher

ARROW

Published in the United Kingdom in 1999 by
Arrow Books

3 5 7 9 10 8 6 4 2

Copyright © Christine Gallagher 1998

Published by arrangement with Carol Publishing Group Inc
of 120 Enterprise Avenue, Secaucus, New Jersey 07094, USA

First published in the United Kingdom in 1999 by
Arrow Books

Arrow Books Limited
The Random House Group Limited
20 Vauxhall Bridge Road, London SW1V 2SA

Random House Australia (Pty) Limited
20 Alfred Street, Milsons Point, Sydney,
New South Wales 2061, Australia

Random House New Zealand Limited
18 Poland Road, Glenfield
Auckland 10, New Zealand

Random House South Africa (Pty) Limited
Endulini, 5a Jubilee Road, Parktown 2193, South Africa

The Random House Group Limited Reg. No. 954009
randomhouse.co.uk

A CIP catalogue record for this book
is available from the British Library

ISBN 0 09 940627 6

Papers used by Random House are natural, recyclable
products made from wood grown in sustainable forests.
The manufacturing processes conform to the environmental
regulations of the country of origin

Typeset in Electra by SX Composing DTP, Rayleigh, Essex
Printed and bound in Great Britain by
Cox & Wyman Ltd, Reading, Berkshire

To all the women who've ever been wronged by a man. In other words, the entire female gender. And with love and kisses to all the men we women have known – the good, the bad and the decidedly ugly.

Contents

Part Three: The Rules of Revenge

Part Four: Catharsis

Part Five: Starting Over

Appendix: A Consumer Guide to Revenge: Products and Services

A word of caution . . . this book is not intended for the mentally unstable. It is intended to amuse and entertain. Neither the author nor the publisher can be held responsible for any action committed by readers of this book. Please don't try to replicate any of the revenge acts that seem blatantly stupid, potentially injurious, disrespectful to human or animal life, or outright dangerous. In other words, don't go out and commit an antisocial act and then say that we made you do it.

PART ONE
Revenge

'Oh people, know that you have committed great sins.
If you ask me what proof I have for these words, I say it
is because I am the punishment of God. If you had not
committed great sins, God would not have sent a
punishment like me upon you.'

GENGHIS KHAN, *Bukhara*

I
Revenge is Sweet

You see your recent ex in a restaurant romantically holding hands with your smiling replacement. You're seething with anger, hoping that the fish the waiter just served him has a nice fat worm in it. Are you big enough to swallow your feelings and send over an expensive bottle of wine, nod, and smile serenely as he looks up to acknowledge it? Of course not. You're human. Once you're past the shock of a nasty break-up, typically the next stage is intense longing for swift and deadly revenge. You find yourself imagining terrible things happening to him. Don't worry, you're not crazy. The desire for revenge is the inevitable next step on the road to recovery.

Revenge is a healthy, natural impulse. And it's a lost art that needs to be mastered by every modern woman. After all, how many of us followed 'the rules' only to find out that the guy they promised would be Prince Charming turned out to be Jerk of the Century? For readers of all ages, married or single, this book is the perfect antidote for any woman reeling in the aftermath of a rotting relationship. It's far healthier than wolfing down an entire chocolate cake and far more affordable than blabbing to a therapist.

Be warned, however. Revenge remains deep in the

shadows of taboo for many people. They'll tell you that revenge is mean, bitchy, small-minded, or politically incorrect. Just smugly remind them that this way of coping with life's problems has been around forever. Revenge features prominently in some of the greatest moments in history and is the emotional core of many great novels and films.

In other words, revenge is not a dirty word. It's a time-honoured tradition. It's a way of bringing the scales of justice back into proper balance, a way of restoring order to the universe. And it's time, girlfriends, to celebrate this underrated tool for self-healing.

REVENGE IS CATHARTIC It's a simple fact of life

that most relationships sooner or later take a nose-dive. The trick is not to let a failed romance take you plummeting down with it. If thoughts of your recent ex make you depressed one second and homicidal the next, then let's fact it, honey, you're a mess. If your heart is as bloody and bruised as roadkill on a motorway at rush hour, then it's time to do something about it. You need to get all that poison out of your system once and for all.

Look at emotional pain as a huge, horrible splinter that can be squeezed out and thrown away. Own up to the fact that you're mad, sad, devastated, and ready for blood. Then channel all those unpleasant feelings into constructive action. In other words, let it all hang out through a fabulous, creative, highly original act of revenge aimed at the one responsible for this mess you are in. Not the Glenn-Close-boils-Michael-Douglas's-kid's-pet-rabbit kind of revenge, but revenge that's healthy, revenge that's cathartic, revenge that helps you get rid of those bad feelings once and for all, lifting you up off the carpet and back out into the world of the living.

AREN'T MEN GREAT? One thing must be made clear up front – this is not a male bashing book. Men are terrific. We all know they perform at least two invaluable functions, one of which is being really good at lugging heavy furniture up flights of stairs. But everyone also knows that they're clumsy when it comes to matters of the heart. As a result, the average female checks into Heartbreak Hotel a staggering seven times in her adult life.

GETTING EVEN For some real-world answers on coping with real-world men read on. We'll explore an abundance of juicy tips on getting even with ex-spouses, ex-lovers, and other undesirables. Together, we'll revel in some of the wonderful ways our sisters have wreaked revenge on the jerks in their lives. We'll look at guidelines for planning and executing a glorious act of revenge on your own bad boy, using some delicious revenge products and services. We'll tackle vital questions such as: When is revenge appropriate? What degree of revenge is called for? What's the difference between constructive and destructive revenge? When is it okay to go 'nuclear'?

Most importantly, we'll move beyond revenge to catharsis and healthier alternatives. We'll redefine revenge as a builder of character, a way to let creativity blossom like it never has before, because revenge done well can be elevated to an art form. Most of all, we'll discover that revenge can make us feel strong, powerful – free! After all, freedom from the fallout of a horrible relationship is the ultimate goal.

2
Revenge Weapons

Before diving into an act of revenge, the well-prepared avenger always makes sure that the punishment fits the crime. It's a good idea to break degrees of revenge down into different levels, depending on whether a minor retaliation, a full-blown assault, or something in between is required.

Your revenge arsenal should similarly be broken down into different levels. Although you might want to come up with your own system, an easy method is to break your weapons down into four categories: slingshots, air rifles, grenades, and nuclear weapons.

- **Slingshots:** These are small acts of revenge. Often humorous, they score high on the fun meter. These are reserved for losers who score high on annoyance but don't have the power to devastate.
- **Air Rifles:** A step up from slingshots, these inflict a little more pain, and the hurt lasts a little longer, but they rarely do lasting damage.
- **Grenades:** Grenades are more damaging, and should be launched in situations more serious than those in which you'd use air rifles or slingshots. For example, your boyfriend has been stolen by a mutual acquaintance.

You and she are not close friends, so it's not a terrible act on her part. It falls more into the underhanded and tacky. So tossing a grenade into their world might be the right choice. You could plant a phoney letter from a male lover in your ex's apartment in a place where *she'll* find it. The letter should be spirited and raunchy, with a reference to your ex's bisexuality.

- **Nuclear Weapons:** Before dropping a nuclear bomb, ask yourself if there is ever justification for ruining someone's life, like irrevocably destroying his reputation by spreading a rumour that he has AIDS. The answer, of course, is yes. But he has to have done a really bad thing to warrant such an extreme response. Harry Truman claimed he dropped the bomb to save the lives of thousands of Americans. In other words, there was a good reason for the death and devastation that was caused in Hiroshima and Nagasaki. Remember, never use nuclear weapons except in the direst of situations, and when you do, use these weapons carefully.

    When might you resort to a nuclear attack? Say your boyfriend's been stolen, and the thief is your best friend – make that your ex-best friend. In a despicable situation like this, you can pull out your big weapons, but be careful. If you do tell the world he has AIDS, this could backfire. After all, he was your lover, too. If the new girlfriend confronts you, act subdued and concerned. Tell her about the relief you felt after getting tested. This will certainly put a crimp in their love life, at the very least.

REVENGE IS POWERFUL A well-executed act of revenge will mark the end of a relationship. In fact, it's usually the final death blow. The relationship will never ever be revived. So be fully aware of the power of revenge before you venture into this domain.

Seen in a positive light, the finality of revenge means that it can also be a powerful tool of liberation. It's a way for you to hoist your own banner of freedom, leaving the dirtbag to rot in the ditch. It will protect you from having to deal with any of his snivelling attempts to reingratiate himself later. The bridges will forever be burned.

PART TWO
Tips on Getting Even

We all love stories of ways in which our creative sisters have plotted revenge on the men in their lives. What follows is an assortment of weird and wonderful revenge tales. While some are only intended to amuse and entertain, others may contain practical tips on how to exorcise your revenge urges once and for all. Remember, the main objective of this book is to get your feelings out in a healthy way – and then get past them.

It should be noted that a few of the stories have been drawn from personal experiences in the phantasmagoric world of romantic relationships. This book may in itself be an act of revenge, for hidden among the anecdotes are true stories of men who did a number on yours truly. Of course it would be much too impolite to reveal their identities – especially the dear who inspired the penile implant story. But to all those ex-amours out there, you know who you are. Thanks, guys, for providing inspiration for this book – not to mention hordes of juicy material.

3
When Divorce Court Doesn't Cut It

Divorce court provides a legal arena for settling accounts between warring spouses. And the rewards are very tangible: houses, money, cars, and other tasty assets. But sometimes material consolation prizes just don't cut it, particularly if your ex-spouse is vindictive or gloating. In these nasty domestic situations, it's not surprising that fantasies of revenge continue to simmer.

THE £50 PORSCHE

A man saw a newspaper ad for an 'almost new' Porsche – price, £50. Thinking it must be a mistake, he hurried over to see the car and was assured by the nice-looking woman who appeared at the door that the price was, indeed, £50. After the man handed over the money and signed the papers, he asked why she was selling it at such a low price. She explained: 'My husband ran off with his secretary a few days ago and left a note instructing me to sell the car and send him the money.'

A NEW HAIRCUT

Most modern men are very concerned that their hair looks good. After all, hair says a lot about a person. There are several amusing tales about women who cut or dyed their husbands' hair while their spouses were fast asleep. One sister sprayed her soon-to-be-ex's sleeping head with a whole can of hair spray. He woke up with a very attractive hair helmet.

Another woman shaved just half of her husband's head while he was frolicking in dreamland. This guy, who was extremely vain, was furious when he woke up and looked in the mirror. Half of his thick wavy hair had simply vanished in the night.

Of course, nocturnal hairstyling should only be done on men who are heavy sleepers. You do not want him to wake up and catch you in the act.

THE INVASION One enterprising divorcée had the misfortune to live on the same street as her ex-husband and she was constantly subjected to seeing him return home with yet another woman with bosoms that far outsized her brain. Meanwhile, the erotic high point of her own life was watching Jimmy Smits take off his shirt every week on *NYPD Blue*.

She decided it was time to change the scenario. She put an ad in the paper announcing that the local chapter of the Devil Worshippers Society would be meeting at her ex's house. The ad noted that new members were welcome and that refreshments would be served.

On the appointed evening, she installed herself in her favourite chair by the window and watched as dozens of people made their way up his driveway that night. There was a lot of green hair, pierced body parts, chains – you get the picture.

THE PLUMMETING MERCEDES
A female resident of the infamous Brentwood community in Los Angeles, packed her soon-to-be-ex-husband's beloved Mercedes with all his expensive clothes. She then drove the car to the top of a hill in the nearby Santa Monica Mountains, where she pushed it off the road and into a deep ravine. While this revenge act must have been incredibly satisfying for the avenger, bear in mind that most men of this income level are well insured and able to quickly and easily replace their belongings.

ALLIE'S REVENGE
When Allie's ex-husband took off with his new girlfriend – for a month in Italy no less – Allie let herself into his new pad and didn't have to wonder for too long whether she should unplug his fridge.

Luckily for Allie, the freezer was full of steaks and shrimp and other potentially smelly items. And, yes, she did leave the fridge and freezer doors wide open. Pulling the plug out of the socket was a small act, but the effect it had when the world traveller returned was by no means minor.

A DECAPITATION
A wealthy Texas sister suffered through a nasty battle in divorce court, and to her amazement, the judge awarded the couple's house, one of those lavish white Southern mansions with a garden full of white Greek statues, to the husband. When she knew her ex was out of town, she hired a stonecutter to come and decapitate all of the statues. This home has since become a popular drive-by attraction.

THE NEW KITCHEN
One woman used her newly expunged husband's credit card to put in an entire new kitchen. Yes, she did get the special marble countertops and the sunken lighting. After all, if a job's worth doing, it's worth doing well. And spending all those hours poring over tile samples and expensive appliance brochures managed to fill her lonely nights at home quite nicely. As the old saying goes, if life gives you lemons, make lemonade. And while you're at it, throw in a kitchen where you can squeeze them.

FLYING JUNK
Avengers might want to take part in a wonderful event called Annual Junk Day, held by Skydive Arizona in America, a skydiving school based near Tucson. Skydivers borne aloft by a cargo plane toss cars, motorcycles, and a host of large objects on to the Sonora Desert from 13,000 feet. It's amazing how demolished things get. And if you're going through a divorce, what a thrilling way to get rid of your ex's belongings. (For more information, see Appendix.)

4
The Philanderer

The philanderer is your primo revenge target. And no one is immune to this most reviled of female adversaries. Even the rich, beautiful, and fabulous suffer the pain and horror of romance turned sour due to infidelity. Look at Liz Taylor, Hillary Clinton, even the glittering Princess Diana. All suffered the same humiliation and betrayal at the hands of dastardly males.

With philanderers, you can let it all hang out with no regrets, because no one more deserves to feel your wrath than the liars and cheats of this world. Save all your juiciest, most diabolical schemes for them.

EXPOSED! There's a wonderful story about a woman
who discovered that her husband was having an affair with his secretary. Worse, it had been going on for a couple of years. All those business trips were really a cover to hide his double life.

The aggrieved wife went to her husband's office when she knew he would be in a board meeting and his secretary would be present, diligently taking notes for her esteemed boss. She walked in and confronted her husband. The entire room froze. The cocky husband turned to his colleagues and said with a smirk, 'I told you she was crazy.' The smile quickly fell off his face when his wife coolly pulled out a realistic-looking toy handgun, pointed it at him, and ordered him to stand up on the table. Seeing that she was deadly serious, he complied. She directed him to first take off his toupee, then remove his false teeth, and finally to drop his pants. She then calmly turned to the secretary and asked, 'Do you still want him now?' With her dignity intact, the wife left the room and went directly to a divorce lawyer.

Needless to say, this put a severe crimp in the affair and was something her husband never ever forgot. Neither did anyone else who was present.

TWO BUNS IN THE OVEN When Jackie discovered her boyfriend was cheating on her, she confronted the other woman. It turned out that he was playing a double game. He had depicted Jackie to the other woman as an unstable old girlfriend who wouldn't stop calling him. Misogyny reared its ugly head again. The two women concocted a devilish plan of revenge. Each went to the slug and told him they were pregnant. After he paid out money to terminate both pregnancies, the women flew off together to the Caribbean for a much-needed holiday.

WHAT A WEDDING This story was passed on by several sources, including my hairdresser, who swears it happened to a friend of his. Is it just a legend, or did it really happen?

It was a beautiful summer day, a perfect day for a wedding. The church was packed with guests. The bride and groom were at the altar ready to say their vows. When the minister asked if there was anyone present who knew of any reason why the couple shouldn't marry, everyone was shocked when the bride spoke up.

With incredible calmness and dignity, she announced that her groom had spent the last night of his bachelorhood in bed with the maid of honour. She then produced an 8 × 10 photograph of the two in *delecto flagrente* and passed it around to the stunned guests.

The bride turned to the red-faced pair and told them to go to hell. She invited all the guests to continue on to the reception, where they had a wild celebration.

AN EYE FOR AN EYE Janey's husband loved to go fishing. She noticed that he was going off on many trips with his unmarried friend Joe, a man who Janey had secretly always found to be very attractive.

One Saturday, when her husband was away for the weekend, Janey ran into Joe at the supermarket. As usual, he was funny and flirtatious. And he certainly wasn't off on any fishing trip. Janey realized that her husband was deceiving her and using Joe as his cover, so she devised a plan of retaliation.

The next time her husband went away for the weekend, Janey invited Joe over to the house under the pretence of having a plumbing problem. She then invited him to go to bed with her. Joe happily accepted the invitation.

Whenever he was away, Janey's husband always called around dinner time, and sure enough, as Janey and Joe rolled around in the sheets, the phone rang. It was Janey's husband, who cheerfully said, 'I'm just calling to say I'm having a good time fishing with Joe.' Janey kept her cool and replied, 'That's nice, dear. Then let me put Joe on the phone. He's right here in bed with me.'

A PIE IN THE FACE

Shoving a pie in your two-timer's face is a simple vaudevillian gesture that is only appropriate in select situations. For example, remember in Nora Ephron's wonderful revenge novel, *Heartburn*, which recounts the story of her painful marriage to Watergate reporter Carl Bernstein? The book itself was a devastatingly public way for Nora Ephron to dish the dirt on her caddish ex-husband. In the film version, the characters are played by Meryl Streep and Jack Nicholson. Meryl has finally had it with Jack's terminal infidelity. During a meal with their friends, she snaps – smashes a key lime pie into his face and walks out. The pie was the perfect dessert course for this relationship as was her skill at whipping up fettucine after late-night sex that had inspired him to propose marriage in the first place.

THE TWISTED SHRINK

Deena, a young copywriter, had a fling with a dashing divorced psychoanalyst, a sensitive and intelligent older man with grey blonde hair and a deep gravelly voice. Deena said he had a real fondness for making love on the couch in his office, a leather antiquey number where his patients poured out their souls.

After a few weeks of candlelit dinners followed by rampant sex on the leather couch, a weird incident occurred. The two were wrapped up in the usual sweaty tangle in his office when a woman came to the locked door and started banging on it, saying she knew he was in there and he had to let her in. The shrink, ever fast on his feet, whispered to Deena that this was a patient who had become very attached to him – he said this was a normal stage in Freudian psychoanalysis.

In the weeks that followed, the shrink was suddenly busy

most evenings. He would call Deena from telephone boxes and explicitly lie about where he was and what he was doing. For example, he called her and said he was at the hospital treating a suicidal patient, yet Deena could hear traffic rushing by in the background. It was almost as if he wanted her to suspect that he was deceiving her. You might wonder why Deena carried on with this nonsense. As she succinctly put it, 'It was a sex thing.'

One day Deena got a call from a woman named Lisa, who accused Deena of being the 'other woman' in *her* relationship. Lisa felt it was time to get it all out on the table. Deena, who had a sick sense of humour and was a big believer in group emotional enemas, agreed to come to Lisa's flat that afternoon a half hour before the shrink was due to pick her up for a date.

Deena arrived at the appointed time. The two women hit it off and shared a pleasant glass of wine. They liked each other and saw the humour in their situation. At four o'clock the doorbell rang and the geriatric Romeo walked in. He was startled at first, but being a suave sophisticate, he kept his cool. The three of them all ended up going out for dinner together. When they parted company at the end of the night, the two women promised to get together again soon, but they never did. Sadly, Lisa made a 180-degree turn and took advantage of Deena's exit from the situation to keep going with the twisted shrink. So much for women sticking together. The moral of the story? Women aren't perfect either.

5
Mysterious Irritations

There are some terrific stories about revenge that have taken the form of a mysterious irritation. This kind of revenge has its roots in ancient biblical traditions. Remember those Old Testament scourges like boils, pestilence, and raining frogs? Modern forms of physically irritating revenge can be just as effective, and they're usually quite gratifying for the avenger. While some of this may seem childish, sometimes childishness can be just what the doctor ordered.

FRIED CHICKEN, ANYONE?
Jane's husband walked out on her shortly after the birth of their second baby. He said he was having a mid-life crisis and needed three months to get himself back together. He moved out to his mother's beach house, taking only his clothes and his surfboard.

Jane soon found out that his 'crisis' was a twenty-three-year-old, tanned and shapely blonde who loved to ski and take trips to Hawaii – in essence, she was all that Jane had been in their younger, premarriage years.

Jane knew that her mother-in-law kept a key under a

plant next to the back door. She went over to the house one day when she knew her husband would be at work, went into the bedroom, and very carefully slit the mattress open. Then she stuffed a fried chicken leg into the gash and sewed it closed. After all, fried chicken was his favourite food.

As the weeks passed, the stench became unbearable. The husband and the beach bunny searched everywhere but they never found the source of the smell.

MORE SMELLY REVENGE There are a number of

smelly revenge stories out there. One girlfriend placed a whole fish under her ex-honey's bed. When he finally found it, it was teeming with maggots. Another woman shoved a hunk of raw meat up her ex's chimney. Not only was it impossible to find the source of the stench, a secondary bonus came in the form of rats who moved into the chimney, where they prospered and multiplied.

What about the resourceful seamstress who broke into her ex-husband's new bachelor pad and sewed tiny popcorn shrimp into the hem of his living room curtains? Rotting fish, as we all know, is truly one of the all-time worst stinks. The husband searched high and low for the source of the odour. He replaced his furniture, and ripped out the carpets and installed new ones at great cost. Finally, at the end of his ropes, he moved. Guess what? Being a cheapskate, he took the curtains with him!

STINK BOMBS Stink bombs are a favourite of twelve-

year-old boys, but hey, if you can't regress to adolescence now, when the heck can you? Stink bombs can be purchased from most joke shops or from mail-order companies. They're cheap – usually around 75p each. If you want to go the distance, make your own. It's easy and it may be a nice release for your vitriol. (See Appendix for purchase information and stink bomb recipes.)

CREEPY-CRAWLY REVENGE The really great
thing about insects is that they reproduce quickly and in vast numbers. Also, most people can't stand them, and have very firm objections about sharing their domiciles with things that have six legs and antennae.

Cockroaches and other beetles are a particular favourite when it comes to creepy-crawly revenge. These little devils can be purchased in many pet shops – they make tasty treats for pet iguanas. (See Appendix.) One woman put cockroaches in a padded envelope, sprinkled in a little sugar to keep them happy, then posted them to her ex.

Susan went one step further. She was well aware of her ex's extreme aversion to all insects. They'd gone camping once and the sap took to his bed for two days afterwards to recover from a sleepless night battling insects, both real and imagined.

Involving insects in her revenge plot seemed like the perfect idea. Susan purchased several dozen cockroaches, then drove over to her ex's home when he wasn't there, opened the letter box, and let the little buggers race gleefully inside to get comfortable in their new residence.

THE ANTS' BREAKFAST Rita's ex had a lovely
green lawn sweeping from the front of his home down to the street. He was particularly proud of this swath of green. He mowed it religiously once a week and put up cute little signs warning the neighbourhood dogs to stay clear. One day Rita sprinkled a jumbo-size box of Frosted Flakes all over his lovely lawn. The result? Within days, the lawn

seemed to have disappeared entirely. It was transformed into a virtual swarm of foraging ants.

PUSSYCATS
Sandra's cheating husband was extremely allergic to cats. After yet another of his amorous adventures, he came home with his tail between his legs (so to speak) and pleaded for another chance. She pretended to soften but told him they had to take things slowly. She'd prefer that he sleep on the sofa the first night. Then she sent him to the supermarket to buy food for breakfast. He cheerfully went, relieved that things were on the upswing between him and his wife.

While he was gone, Sandra enticed two mangy cats from the neighbourhood into the house and rubbed them all over the sofa and sheets. The next morning, her hubby woke up in agony. His eyes were swollen shut. There were welts all over his body. As subtle as she could be, she said, 'You wanted pussy, you got it.'

ANIMAL MAGNETISM
When Laurie found out that her boyfriend was a dog – make that a dog in perpetual heat – calling on the animal kingdom to help her give him his comeuppance seemed the perfect way to go.

Through a dog breeder she knew, she purchased a hormone 'harvested' from an ovulating bitch (apparently it's used to help reluctant male dogs get in the mood for love), then she rubbed the hormone into her boyfriend's shoe leather.

The next day he hurried as usual along the busy London streets on the way to his office. And guess what? Every single male dog he passed tried to mount him. The coup de grace occurred when he passed a dog walker who was walking a dozen dogs. The dogs went into a frenzy. He was the belle of the ball.

OLD SPICE REVISITED

Speaking of female scents, there was a ruling in France some time ago that if you were wearing a certain famous perfume that began with the letter 'G', you couldn't enter a public restaurant. The perfume is so pungent that many find it offensive. Worse, you can't wash the scent away completely without scraping off your top layer of skin.

How about spraying this perfume on all of his suits? Wool is particularly porous so apply it heavily. But don't hold back – empty the whole bottle.

NIGHT BLOOMERS

After her wretched ex-husband remarried and had the cheek to move into Gretchen's neighbourhood, she decided to leave the newlyweds a little welcoming gift.

One day when there was no one home, Gretchen planted a night-blooming olive tree right outside their bedroom window. This plant exudes an intense aroma on summer nights, cloying and sweet like a French whorehouse.

Being new to the house, the couple did not realize that a strange new plant had suddenly appeared in their garden. But as summer approached and they began to sleep with the windows open, they grew increasingly aware of the overpowering presence.

BELOW THE BELT

Sally works as a graphic artist at a greeting card factory where she became friendly with a new neighbour, Kathy. Kathy was newly divorced, unemployed, and worried about her future. Sally felt sorry for her and helped her to get a job in the accounts department at her company. She even offered to let Kathy ride with her to and from work.

A few months later, Sally began to suspect, and soon confirmed, that Kathy was having an affair with none other than Sally's own husband!

When Sally drove Kathy home the next day, she invited herself in for coffee. While Kathy was in the shower, Sally found her underwear and rubbed poison ivy into the crotches of all her panties. The next morning she deliberately stood Kathy up and didn't drive her to work. Later in the day, she sauntered down to the accounts department where she discovered that Kathy had gone to casualty.

6
Surprise, Surprise

Surprises always have a lot of impact – surprise gifts, surprise parties, or surprising acts of revenge. This is an area where so many women have revealed themselves to be incredibly resourceful by concocting surprises that their exes will probably never forget.

THE £10,000 PHONE BILL
A man unceremoniously dumps his live-in girlfriend. He tells her he's leaving town for two weeks and he wants her and all her belongings out of the flat before he returns.

When he comes back, he enters the flat cautiously, worried his girlfriend may have trashed the place, or worse, may still be there. All seems quiet, that is, until he notices the phone is off the hook and there's a strange voice on the other end speaking with a thick Australian accent. When his next phone bill arrives, he discovers that his former lover had called the time information number in Queensland, Australia, and left the phone off the hook. The phone bill ran to thousands of pounds. (See Appendix for several useful Australian phone numbers.)

CLASSIFIED ADS

Although newspaper ads that include your ex's phone number involve a small expense, they can be quite gratifying, especially if they trigger a flood of responses. For example, you might offer his baby-sitting services at £3 an hour.

A favourite of mine is the story of the woman who put a classified ad in the local paper offering an incredibly cheap rental of a magnificent house. She included her ex's home and office telephone number, noting that applicants should 'call anytime, day or night'.

PRANKS

There's a big difference between an act of revenge and a prank. The motive of the avenger is to get justice, while the motive of the prankster is to annoy people for his or her own amusement. Pranks are usually lightweight actions without much lasting impact. An example of a prank is that old college favourite where you place a brown paper bag full of dog pooh on your mark's doorstep and set it on fire, ring the doorbell, and then make a fast exit. The mark will open the door, see the flames, and hopefully try to stomp them out – getting pooh all over his shoes.

If a simple prank will meet your revenge needs, try to be creative. Give it a personal touch. For example, if your ex has a hot tub where he likes to entertain the ladies, how about tossing in several live crabs – the kind with big snapping claws?

THE CEMENT CAR

A woman became ill at her office and came home early. She was surprised to see her husband's cement lorry parked in the driveway alongside a nifty red convertible sports car. She tiptoed around the house, found the bedroom curtains closed, and heard sounds of passionate lovemaking coming from within. Without disturbing the happy couple, she calmly climbed into the cab of the cement lorry, backed it up, and deposited the entire load of cement into the sports car.

THE PINK SWIMMING POOL
Whenever Gwen thought of her ex-husband bringing dates home to frolic in his beautiful new swimming pool, she seethed with anger: They'd never been able to afford a pool when they were together. She came up with the perfect antidote to her fury. She arranged with a contractor to drain the pool and paint it hot pink. Imagine her ex's surprise the next time he showed up for a swim date with a young honey.

CLOTHES MAKE THE MAN
Eve's soon-to-be ex was a clothes hound – and also a corporate executive who had to look sharp every day. So Eve gave him a whole new look by sending all his trousers to the dry cleaners with the direction to shorten the legs by three inches. When they came back, she hung them in his wardrobe as usual. Imagine his shock and surprise the next morning when it seemed that he had grown three inches overnight.

Another of our sisters got into her ex-boyfriend's under-wear drawer and sewed up all the flies. She figured that with luck he wouldn't notice her handiwork when he first put on the underwear, but once he got to the men's room . . . talk about a quick fumble. She revelled in the mental picture of him standing at the urinal with his boxers bunched around his ankles – and the CEO walking in.

PLEASANTLY PLUMP

One woman wreaked glorious revenge on her commitment-phobic ex-boyfriend by turning up pregnant at one of his favourite restaurants. She stuffed a pillow under her clothes and acted casual and serene. She also had the foresight to have her phone number changed so he couldn't reach her to alleviate his anxiety about whether or not he was the baby's father.

7
Dial-a-Revenge

The telephone can be an invaluable tool for any avenger. Use it to torment him – especially in the wee hours of the night. You can also use the phone to dial up a wide range of wonderful products and services that will aid you in torturing him. The advantages of letting your fingers do your avenging are several. You can do phone-revenge in the privacy of your own home, and with the touch of a few buttons, you can order a cornucopia of products and services that will leave an unforgettable impression on your ex-lollipop.

DEAD FLOWER DELIVERY
An innovative company in America has sprung up that offers this invaluable service. You can order over the phone or via your computer. Choose from a range of drab dead flower bouquets, which you can have delivered to your sweetheart along with a choice personal message. Other selections include a sombre funeral wreath, black roses, and a box of melted chocolates. Kudos to this entrepreneur for providing this fabulous service. (See Appendix for information on purchasing revenge products.)

SPIRITUAL ADVISERS
You might consider calling the Hare Krishna folks and giving them his name, address, and phone number. Tell them he wants to make a big donation, and make an appointment for them to visit his office. Hopefully they'll draw a lot of attention to themselves and to him as they enter.

The same could be done with Jehovah's Witnesses. Request the special weekly visit package, which they're always very happy to deliver.

PORN VIDEOS
Jenna called her ex's office, pretending she was an assistant at a video shop. She left a message with his secretary explaining that all the X-rated videos he'd rented were long overdue and should be returned immediately. You could do the same with a well-timed call to your ex's home when you know his new girlfriend might answer.

DIAL-A-GIFT
There are a host of stories about our sisters ordering outrageous gifts to be delivered to their ex's homes. There are the old standbys like ordering a dozen pizzas to be delivered when you know he's home, as well as more creative ideas, like sending a truckload of rocks, a coffin, and even fifty pounds of raw meat.

How about putting his name on the mailing list for the armed forces? He'll be swamped with phone calls and post. Or the Psychic Friends Network in America? Sign him up – at his expense, of course.

V.D. ALERT
This is a good one. Enlist a pal to leave the following message on your ex's answering machine:

'This is Dr. Smith. We have a female patient down here at our clinic. She has a rare but highly contagious venereal disease and has listed you as one of her sexual partners. Please call us back at –' Then make a lot of static and clicking, as if the line went dead. This is guaranteed to drive him bonkers as he tries to find Dr. Smith (use a common name like this). Chances are he'll go through a battery of tests to track down the rare venereal disease.

THE FIVE POUND NOTE
One woman came up with a deliciously nasty plan. She wrote on the border of a five pound note in tiny letters: 'Men seeking men. For a good time, call (her ex's phone number).' This is an annoyance that will last as long as that five pound note is in circulation – the gift that keeps on giving.

THE 3 A.M. PHONE CALL
Phone your ex every night at 3 A.M. and hang up. Alternatively, page him and leave the number of a phone sex line. One creative friend of ours called her ex in the middle of the night and disguised her voice, saying she was calling from casualty. She said they had a woman in labour who had named him as the father and he had to come down immediately.

DIAL-A-PENIS
All women know that many men are insecure about their penile qualities. The poor dears worry about their comparative characteristics, especially in terms of size. They sometimes reveal this to their girlfriends, probably hoping to be reassured that they are indeed up to par.

Alicia's ex had revealed penile insecurity on a number of occasions, so after their nasty break-up, as she pondered retribution, going for this weak spot (the bull's-eye, so to speak) seemed like an excellent idea.

She called a plastic surgeon specializing in penis enhancement and left a message with her ex-darling's work number. She also requested written materials to be posted to his office. Knowing his insecurity, she knew that even if he managed to keep it together when his secretary gave him the phone message, inside he'd be dying.

DIAL-A-STRIPPER One woman who was aware of
her ex's business schedule hired a male stripper to crash his next high-level business meeting and deliver a message to him: 'Bruce says to tell you he still loves you.'

She revelled in the vision of her open-mouthed ex trying to talk his way out of the interruption to a table full of conservative colleagues in business suits.

Another woman took this juicy scenario one step further. She hired a male stripper to go to her boyfriend's boss's home, compliments of the boyfriend.

DIAL-A-STINK One sister ordered a truckload of
manure to be delivered to her ex-honey's home. She gave specific instructions as to where she wanted it dumped – blocking the entrance to the driveway. This is a personal favourite. Subtle, direct, and makes its point.

THE PHANTOM JOB OFFER Our good friend
Cynthia had finally had it with her loud-mouthed egotistical boyfriend, a corporate executive, and plotted her revenge to capitalize on his irritating personality. She had a friend call and leave a message on his answering machine offering the worm a fantastic job with a huge raise at a

competitor's headquarters.

Knowing of his big mouth and tendency to blow his own horn, she knew he'd immediately brag about the offer to his colleagues. And as he rode the wave of self-inflation, she thought he might even quit his job. She was right. When he called back to accept the offer, he found himself on the phone with a dog-grooming business.

8
Mail Revenge

The Royal Mail is a revenge mechanism that is accessible to everyone, and it can be utilized in all sorts of innovative ways. Warning: keep it fun; don't do anything that might subject you to charges of postal fraud; and be careful not to leave a trail of incriminating evidence. Here are some tips:

- Never sign your name.
- Never use your old typewriter, the one with the broken S and T keys.
- Never post something to him from your neighbourhood if you don't want him to know that you are the sender. You might consider enlisting an anonymous remailer who will send your missile from a distant location. (See Appendix for details.)
- And never, never lick a stamp. There's a famous case where a woman was arrested for murder simply on the basis of the DNA found on the saliva on the back of a postage stamp. So beware – and be careful.

JUNK MAIL
Junk mail provides an easy way to get revenge. As a weapon, it rates as a slingshot, at most, a

grenade. Here are some of the ways women have used junk mail to torment their tormentors.

One clever woman got her ex's name on a mailing list of sperm donors. Once you're on this list, it's hard to get off, so to speak. A similar option would be to call a sperm bank in your area and offer his services. Request that all the sign-up information be posted to him pronto.

In a related story, Ellen's boyfriend idealized his parents' marriage. In his opinion, they had the perfect relationship. As he put it, his dad was always the pilot and his mum the copilot. Once Ellen realized her boyfriend was getting ready to buckle her into his cockpit, she made a fast exit. As a parting gift, she put the 'enlightened one' on a mailing list for mail-order brides.

Other mailing lists you might consider are those for twelve-step programmes. Endless junk mail from these organizations can be very embarrassing, especially when sent to his workplace.

Another good network to plug him into might be an extreme right wing group. Once he's on their mailing list, he'll be able to enjoy all sorts of startling post and perhaps even a surprise visit or two.

MAGAZINE HELL A benign and gentle librarian somehow got tangled up with a character who did a use-and-dump number on her.

As she sat at her desk in the library one day, fuming over the whole humiliating ordeal, her eyes fell upon the stacks of periodicals. An idea formed. Now this is quite tame, but for her, it was gloriously vengeful. She pulled out the little order form in every single magazine. Then she filled out every one with his name and address and popped them into the post box. She relished the thought of him being buried in junk mail and subscription bills.

PORNO PEN PALS

PORNO PEN PALS This one comes from a friend with a great sense of humour, and like me, she believes that revenge is an excellent way to equalize a wrong-doing on a cosmic level. She posted an ad in a porno magazine, the kind that is full of those blurry black-and-white photographs of 'the naughty bits', as Monty Python called them. The ad, ostensibly sent by her ex, was very polite and earnest in tone. It expressed interest in having correspondence with a pen pal, a prison inmate who is preferably bisexual. The ad generously allowed for the consideration of death row inmates. It ended with a request for applicants to send photographs, preferably full frontal shots.

Another pal happened to have a picture of her ex-sweetheart naked. They'd been sunbathing on a nude beach in the south of France, at least that was the story she told us. She cropped the photo to emphasize his 'features' and sent it to a porno magazine to post in the personals. She included the ex's phone number and implored interested parties to call day or night.

A PERMANENT GOODBYE Sex and death. In the big picture, these are life's driving forces, right? And sometimes the two even go together very nicely. A woman with a deliciously macabre sense of humour gave her squeeze the big heave-ho in a very innovative fashion. She purchased a memorial urn and put a cheerful little note inside giving him the big elbow. She then sent it to his office for him to open in front of his colleagues.

SPECIAL LOVE GIFTS Most cities have those tawdry sex shops that sell all kinds of grotesque sex aids and numbingly crass sex toys, most of which are major turnoffs for women. Visit a sex shop in your area and select something that you're pretty sure would be offensive to anyone of your sex. An example might be a nurse's outfit complete with crotchless panties. Send it to his new girlfriend with his compliments. She might just get so mad she'll break up with him. Of course, this could all backfire and lead to a sex fest.

BROWN-NOSING HIS BOSS This is an underhanded trick but it definitely should be part of your arsenal for extreme situations. Enroll his boss in a gay rights club. Be sure to ask them to send as much written material as possible. Ask for his name to be put on all relevant mailing lists, and make sure they include your ex's name as the referral, just to be sure he knows who's responsible.

PENISES BY MAIL Mail-a-Penis is sooo nasty, but good for a chuckle. While you're in that sex shop, look around for a penis extender. Yes, they do exist. In certain African countries they use long gourds, but these will be hard to find in your local supermarket. Anyway, once you've located the extender, ask the sales assistant to post it to your ex. To add salt to the wound, sign the card, 'from all your exes'.

If you want to avoid the sex shop scene, simply have information on penile implants posted to his office. To locate companies which supply these intriguing little devices, go to your local newsagent and look in the health section for magazines geared to diabetics. Most include advertisements for penile aids.

SURPRISE GIFTS This seems obvious, but you could post all kinds of goodies to your ex. We've heard of people posting gross gifts like vomit, excrement, even dead animals. Now we're all probably above stooping to such childish levels, right? But you might take the basic idea and add your own creative flourish. For example, one woman posted her departed spouse a 'sample' of some mail-order herbs. He fancied himself a gourmet cook and loved to swagger around the kitchen whipping up dishes and adding a dash of herbs à la Nigel Slater.

A month later, she followed up by sending a note on black-bordered stationery, apparently from a pet cemetery, asking if he'd mistakenly received the container of little Fido's ashes. This is a true story. Honest.

9
Fiscal Revenge

How many wives, when faced with an impending divorce, make the necessary transition from teary depression to seething anger by maxing out their soon-to-be ex's credit cards? Hitting a man where it hurts the most – in the wallet – can be a very satisfying experience.

Caution: check with your credit card company before seizing on this mode of instant gratification. Some wily spouses have been known to anticipate this kind of offence and have protected their butts by cancelling their cards, leaving the poor wife with an act of revenge that explodes right in her face.

Also take note that the times are a-changing. Gone are the old guarantees where wives automatically win houses, assets, and alimony. The quest for equality has reached the divorce courts. So tread carefully. Men can win big too.

There are some awful cases where women are paying alimony to deadbeat ex-spouses. Liz Taylor pays her recent ex a huge amount of money every month. In a lesser known case, Catherine, a highly paid advertising executive in a leading agency, was married to a struggling writer. When they had a child, she offered to work full-time to support the household while he wrote and supervised the child's care.

Of course it didn't work out that way. She ended up working like a dog, paying for a full-time nanny and taking charge of all the child's needs, like doctor appointments, nursery school, and more, while he did nothing.

Their marriage became very strained and eventually they divorced. He then had the incredible gall to sue her for spousal support. Unbelievably, he won. Soon after, he got his big break and sold a screenplay for a huge amount of money. Worse, he even tried to hide his income from the court.

Catherine's revenge was perfect. She had long tired of the rat race at work, fending off the up-and-coming junior executives who were all eager to grab her position. One day she quit her job. After years of intense work, she was happy to fill her days painting, doing ceramics and spending time with her son. She returned to court and had her fiscal arrangement with her ex restructured. Now she receives the substantial alimony she justly deserves.

A WHOLE NEW YOU There's nothing like a new wardrobe to lift a woman out of a post-relationship funk. One jilted wife moved really fast from spending entire days languishing in despair to virtually taking up residence in the local shopping centre where, shallow though it may be, she shed her victimhood and achieved a new kind of empowerment by going on a spending spree with her husband's credit card that would put Ivana Trump to shame.

HELP THE HOMELESS Another woman caught in the wake of a disastrous relationship killed two birds with one stone by merging the act of revenge with a lovely philanthropic gesture: she bought new clothes for the entire local homeless community.

NEW BODY PARTS

Some women use plastic surgery to relieve their trauma. This can actually work out quite well. If you have a facelift or a nose job, you can hang out in a convalescent home for a few days and have some time to pamper yourself before heading back to the world with a whole new lease of life, not to mention a whole new face.

No one is suggesting that changing one's appearance will change one's life. We women are not that superficial, are we? The point is, if you are compelled to get new breasts, why not do it now while *he* can pay for it? And think of how you can gloat when he runs into the newly curvaceous you on the arm of a doting new beau.

DINNER RESERVATIONS

Some expensive restaurants now have a policy that if you make a reservation and don't show up, you have to pay a penalty. After all, they're losing revenue when they hold an empty table for a no-show.

How about making reservations at all the best restaurants in your city in his name and leaving his credit card number? This can drag on nicely, as it will probably take a while for all those charges to show up on his statement.

CANCELLED CREDIT CARDS AND PHONE CARDS

We all know how annoying and embarrassing it can be when we go to pay for something with a credit card only to have the assistant or waiter hand it back, saying it's been declined. Why not cancel all his credit cards, especially if he's the type that never carries much cash?

Cancelling his phone cards can also be extremely irritating, especially if he's one of those guys who make a lot of business calls while travelling.

FREE PHONE CALLS This one is nasty. One woman
vented all her anger one day by running around an airport
writing her ex's telephone charge card number on as many
public phones as possible. Whenever the feelings returned,
she'd pull over to a pay phone and scrawl the number.
Voilà. Her bad thoughts were exorcized.

THE INLAND REVENUE Involving the Inland
Revenue, or any government agency for that matter, is only
advised when you are legally free and clear of your ex and
his affairs. But there have been instances where spurned
wives and girlfriends have done their civic duty and called
their local Inland Revenue office (see Appendix) to alert
them to their ex's financial misdeeds, which can range
from bending the truth to outright criminal behaviour. Be
aware that some Inland Revenue infractions will lead to
prison terms, and if your ex is cute, that stint in prison may
turn into a whole lot more than he bargained for.

FAREWELL GIFTS We all love gifts, and he will too.
Until, of course, he realizes they've been sent c.o.d., or that
a flood of mail-order packages has added a sizeable chunk
to his credit card statement. Send him things you know
he'll always cherish like tacky figurines, velvet paintings,
fluffy toilet seat covers – you get the picture.

PURPLE HAZE

Sometimes a woman just has to make a statement. Loraine was sick to death of her boyfriend, whom she'd nicknamed the grey man. She would complain to her friends because he was ultra-conservative and never wanted to have any fun. The deal breaker came when Loraine won a trip to Tahiti in a sweepstake competition. The grey man said he couldn't take the time off from work to accompany her, but he had an important business trip coming up in Birmingham. He asked her if she would rather go with him instead.

For Loraine, this was the last straw. After he'd left town and before she set off alone to the South Seas, she devised an appropriate parting gift. She called a painter and arranged to have his house painted bright purple, and she paid with his credit card. (She'd had the foresight to jot the number down one night in a restaurant.) The boyfriend was so stunned when he came back to his house, he almost had a heart attack. What was worse, the people in the neighbourhood were up in arms because of this aesthetic violation. Someone had even called a local TV news crew to alert them to the brouhaha. Who could that have been?

ARMANI BARGAINS

This is by no means original, but many women have disposed of their ex's clothes by going to car boot sales in which passersby are treated to all sorts of bargains, like £1 for a suit. When he shows up to pick up his wardrobe you can thrust a pile of grubby pound coins into his hand and say the sale was very successful, thank you.

10
His Beloved Car

Men love their cars. That's a fact of life. Their cars are often an extension of their masculinity and libido, so targeting revenge in this arena can be particularly effective.

OUR FEATHERED FRIENDS
Kylie knew her ex-beau parked his car near a park, so she took advantage of the location, which was densely populated with birds. She sprinkled his beloved BMW with bread crumbs. The birds loved it. They even left behind a multitude of hard-to-remove gestures of appreciation. As we all know, bird droppings can do a number on car paint. You may also try using fish oil to attract birds. This is the better choice on windy days.

If there are no birds around, try smearing honey all over the car, especially if it's parked anywhere near an ants' nest.

SABOTAGE!
There are, of course, lots of ways to trash someone's car. Pouring sugar or sand in the petrol tank is an oldie but goodie. In a similar vein, sprinkling acid on the soft top of your ex's convertible would definitely put a

wrinkle in his day. A mild assault would be to replace the petrol cap with a lockable one – but you keep the key, of course. For the interior buy skunk scent and inject it into the vent system of the car.

A young woman in Minneapolis covered every inch of her man's car with shaving cream in the dead of a Minnesota winter. At first glance he assumed it was snow, but when he touched it, it was rock solid like a big meringue.

WHERE'S THE WINDEX? Samantha came up
with a similar ultra-annoying tactic. On a cold winter's night she sought out her darling's car and covered all the windows with Vaseline. Vaseline also hardens nicely in cold temperatures. The next morning it was impossible to remove. Equally effective, by the way, is black shoe polish.

THE MYSTERIOUS RATTLE One resourceful young
woman was very handy with tools. After her boyfriend dumped her because, as he said, he finally knew what love was (with someone else, of course), she carefully unscrewed one of the plastic door panels inside his car. Then she inserted a ball bearing (a key or any small metallic object will work fine) and screwed the panel back into place.

Young Casanova was nearly driven crazy by the mysterious rattle that plagued his beloved car. He took it to mechanic after mechanic but no one could locate the source of the problem. Finally, he took the car back to the dealer and screamed bloody murder till they promised to dismantle the car and find the source of the problem. Behind the door panel they discovered the ball bearing along with a nice hand-written note left by Miss Resourceful, which read: 'Congratulations! You finally found it!'

STINKMOBILE
Smelly revenge also works well in the car. Once, a pound of raw liver accidentally slipped out of a grocery bag and sat in the sun all day on the fabric-covered rear seat of my car. So I feel personally qualified to attest to the effect of direct sunlight on raw meat, especially when it is in a small unventilated space like a car. When one woman told how she taped strips of bacon under her ex's driver's seat, it was not difficult to imagine the results. Bacon's a good choice because it's flat and not easily detected if someone were to peer under the seat looking for the source of the horrible stink.

Another sister took a carton of milk and carefully poured it all over the carpeted floor of her ex's car. This is especially effective in the summer.

Yet another variation involves putting chicken giblets in a jar, screwing the lid on tight, and then leaving the jar in the boot of the offender's car on a hot sunny day. The result? The jar will explode, splattering chicken guts all over the interior of the boot.

AQUAMOBILE
There was a girl in my high school in America who trashed her boyfriend's baby blue Corvette by slipping a hose in through a cracked window and filling the car with water. She had just found out that he had impregnated one of the cheerleaders in the back seat of this very same car. Clearly, this was some kind of purging and cleansing ritual. One thing's for sure – it purged him from her life for good.

HOLD THE HANDSHAKE
A popular Halloween prank in the States is to squirt shaving cream under car door handles. Adapt this for your departed ex's car. A mild

version would be to smear cake icing under the door handles. A more lethal version – doggie pooh. Imagine him cavalierly opening the car door for his date only to get a handful of what one besotted poodle owner I know calls 'Fifi's little chocolates'.

PSYCHEDELIC CAR A smart young secretary made
the fatal error of having an affair with her boss, a successful corporate lawyer. Eventually the affair became too complicated – he was, after all, married with two children – and he very abruptly dumped her. Even harder to swallow was that he expected her to continue doing her job as if nothing had ever happened.

The secretary knew that filing a complaint against her boss would be tricky since their relationship was consensual. She also knew that such matters could get messy if any of the men in power chose to close ranks and blame her. So she turned her predicament into an opportunity. She approached personnel and asked for a promotion, something she'd been wanting to do for some time. To her pleasure, she got a better position in the company, far away from lover-boy.

To exact her revenge, she paid someone to paint his car while it was parked in the company car park. He had a plush Mercedes sedan which he used to transport clients to lunches and court appointments. Imagine his surprise when he came down to the car park with his clients to find his car had a sixties-style psychedelic paint job complete with flames licking along the side panels. It didn't take a lot of brainpower for him to figure out who was responsible, but she knew he could do nothing about it without blowing his cover.

SERIAL REVENGE

It's unfortunate when your significant other lives close by, especially after a relationship goes down the toilet. It galled Maggie to see her boyfriend out bike riding with the woman he'd been secretly seeing throughout their relationship.

Maggie decided to make the most of his close proximity and turn it into an advantage. She strolled over to where his car was parked one evening, took a wrench out of her pocket, and loosened his number plates so that they would fall off, not right away, but when he picked up speed, hopefully on the motorway. We all know what a pain it is to have to go and get new plates, and she knew how much this would get to him, since he was a very impatient man.

Maggie, however, didn't stop there. She waited a couple of weeks and repeated the act all over again. In fact, she did it several times until eventually he couldn't take it anymore and had the bolts permanently welded.

DONATE TO CHARITY

In the States, certain charities are delighted to accept old cars as donations. They will even come and tow your heap away and sell it to benefit their cause. You're relieved of the bother of selling the car, and you get a nice fat tax deduction.

Consider utilizing this service in plotting your revenge act. Call a charity and say that you and your husband are indebted to their cause. Fabricate a personal connection to the charity. For example, if it's a cancer charity, say your beloved aunt just died of cancer, or whatever. This will explain your generosity. Say you'd like to offer a sizeable contribution through the donation of your (his) car. Ask to take advantage of their free towing service. Give them the location of the car, thank them politely, and then hang up. This will only work if your name is on the registration document (it can be in both of your names), and you have to be there to hand it over, so plan ahead.

SPANK THAT MONKEY There's a man in our
office building, a known ladykiller who drives an eye-catching red Jaguar. One of his multiple girlfriends won my admiration when she slipped into the office car park and put a note under his windscreen wiper that read: 'Will be back soon. Gone off to masturbate.'

This was in full view of everyone who drove in and out of the car park that day. Even the valets were amused, especially when lover boy strode out and saw it.

FREE ADVERTISING I recently saw a car that had
the words 'Registered Sex Offender' spray-painted on the back. Obviously the driver had not noticed it before getting into the car. I laughed, knowing this was probably the handiwork of a disgruntled sister.

A more elaborate version might be to tape a sign to the rear bumper that reads: 'I'm a Jerk. Please Honk and Give Me the Finger.' Chances are he'll drive off without seeing it and there will be plenty of drivers out there who'll gladly accept his invitation.

A more sinister variation was told to me by an American friend. A woman in her town slapped KKK stickers all over the rear bumper of her husband's car. He'd done something really bad to warrant this extreme response: he'd taken up with their teenage baby-sitter. Anyway, he didn't notice her handiwork and got beaten up. Many people in the town felt he deserved it, since the baby-sitter was by no means his first foray out of the marital compound. Of course, the ending of this story could have been much worse so we are by no means suggesting that anyone copy it.

11
Home, Sweet Home

Still have his key? Excellent! This opens up a world of revenge opportunities for you in his home sweet home. Of course, you have to shape your plan to the particular guy in your life. There's no point thinking up the awful things you could do to his kitchen if the only time he goes in there is to stuff a pizza box in the bin.

BALD AND BEAUTIFUL

Notwithstanding the appeal of Patrick Stewart or Yul Brynner, most men would rather be dragged stark naked behind a galloping horse than wake up one morning to find themselves as bald as a newly laid egg – especially if the new look is something that occurs very rapidly and without warning.

Knowing the effect this has on men, Nina tried it out on her lying, cheating boyfriend. She went into his shower, emptied his shampoo bottle, and filled it with hair remover – and she did it on a weekday, which meant that he had to go to work in his shiny new state. Since hair grows slowly, usually an average of half an inch a month, the impact of Nina's action lasted a very long time. And since he was vain and prone to worry about his appearance, it was an extremely effective way of paying him back in spades.

For the Ronald McDonald look, use bright orange hair dye instead of hair remover. Be sure to get the kind that doesn't wash out easily.

THE SEDUCTIVE COOK Brad was one of those cynical guys who thought he knew all the ways to win women over. He even bragged to his girlfriend, Martha, that before they met he had gone to a relationship seminar that was packed with women who were single but didn't want to be. Brad told the psychologist speaker and everyone in the room that he had a hard time meeting women. He added that he had just purchased a beautiful beachfront home and looked forward to the day he could share it with a mate. During the break, hordes of women descended on him. He walked out with a pocketful of phone numbers. As Brad told Martha this story, chuckling over the gullibility of women, Martha realized that she never wanted to see this jerk again.

After they'd broken up, she saw him at the supermarket. Judging by the items in his shopping trolley – the baby greens, the fresh berries – she knew he was about to give one of his seductive dinners. Inviting women over to his flat for a cosy dinner at home was one of his ace cards. Like many men, Brad knew the power of this tactic. Women love men who cook, and for men, it's an easy way of luring women within kissing distance of the bedroom. Martha herself had fallen for Brad's ploy before she wised up to the weasel. She remembered how cute he'd looked in his little apron. At the time she thought that since he wore the apron so easily, with no self-consciousness, he must be a real man.

As she watched him squeezing the cantaloupes, a devilish little revenge idea came to Martha. She decided to put a little wrinkle in his romantic evening.

She dumped her shopping, found his key, which was still in the glove compartment of her car, and raced over to his flat. In the kitchen she carefully heated liver of sulphur and candle wax until they were melted together and then poured the result on the heating coils of the stove. The beauty of it was that Brad had no inkling of Martha's revenge until he started cooking, his admiring date standing in the doorway, a glass of wine in her hand. As the substance heated up, it exuded the most revolting stink imaginable. The date's admiration swiftly turned to repulsion and she hightailed out of the flat faster than a bullet out of a gun. Poor Brad hadn't a clue what had happened and why his culinary creation smelled like a hippo pond.

KUDZU REVENGE No, kudzu is not a weird ritual
from Borneo involving small coconuts, machetes, and high-pitched screams. Nor is it some £1.99 lunch special at the sushi counter in your local shopping centre.

Kudzu is a voracious, extremely invasive vine. It can grow as fast as a foot a day. Introduced to America by Japanese gardeners at the Centennial Exposition in Philadelphia in 1876, it was embraced by Americans as a fast-spreading ornamental ground cover. Known these days as the 'vine that ate the South' or the 'mile-a-minute vine', it has now devoured seven million acres of the southeastern United States and is an out-of-control menace. What's worse, it's extremely hard to kill.

Sound like a good revenge tool? I thought so too. And I was thrilled when Sandy, who has a flair for the horticultural, suggested this particular revenge plot. Imagine your ex going on a long holiday with his new girlfriend. Better still, he's headed off on an extended honeymoon. As soon as he leaves, you go over to his house, plant kudzu all over the place and leave the rest to Mother Nature.

Fast forward now. Imagine the look on his face when he finds that his house and garden have become one big knot of dense green foliage, and even better – this weird topiary nightmare has spread down the chimney to swallow up the interior.

Consider this good fodder for fantasy. If you ever did this for real, chances are you'd be in serious violation of plant control regulations. So don't say you weren't warned.

LIPSTICK EVIDENCE
Some people say that a man who cheats on his partner will most likely cheat again. Lou knew that the woman who'd stolen her husband and was now living with him must sometimes wonder if he would eventually cheat on her too.

Lou preyed on this probable insecurity by giving the thieving woman a taste of her own bitter medicine. She did something many of us might find bizarre or compulsive, but for Lou, it was helpful in catapulting her back into her life.

From time to time, Lou would quietly let herself into her ex's home and put lipstick marks on his shirt collars. This was how she herself had first discovered that her husband was cheating on her. And when the new woman discovered the lipstick, the snake's pleas of innocence fell on deaf ears. Liars often carry this burden – nobody ever really trusts them again. Lou succeeded in breaking the pair apart, something that gave her no small dose of satisfaction.

JUMPING BEANS
As a child I was fascinated by those little packages of so-called Mexican jumping beans. My brothers and I quickly tired of watching the little buggers jump around (lurching would be a better description), so we tossed them under the bed and forgot about them. Imagine our horror when the beans had the

bad manners to hatch. They turned into incredibly huge and ugly brown moths, the likes of which we had never seen.

This memory sparked a revenge idea. Check your local joke shop for Mexican jumping beans. Buy a package and leave them in your ex's home in a warm secluded corner, like behind the kitchen stove or in the airing cupboard. After all, he always wanted pets.

A TRAVELLING COMPANION
How can you totally humiliate him and perhaps even wreck his career? Does he go on a lot of business trips? Before he leaves on a trip, especially if he's travelling with an important client, take a dildo and wrap it well with tin foil and black tape. Then slip it into one of the side pockets of his suitcase – one that you're pretty sure he won't use.

When he goes through airport security, guess what? This missile-shaped object will show up nicely on the X-ray screen. He will no doubt be subjected to all kinds of scrutiny.

RUBBISH IN, RUBBISH OUT
At first Nancy thought her husband was an angel for helping the widow next door whenever she needed a man's help with home repairs – but when Nancy caught them nude together in the widow's swimming pool, the angel quickly turned red and sprouted horns. Nancy went home and called a locksmith to immediately change the locks. Then she shoved all her husband's belongings into black plastic bin liners and left them out on the pavement.

Sometimes a fast resolution like this is the best way to go. The guy, of course, pleaded, 'Let's at least talk about it.' But in a case like this, what's there to talk about?

SINGIN' IN THE RAIN

Unlike the rainstorm in the film, in this story the storm took place in a guy's living room. But not just any old living room, one sumptuously furnished with deep leather couches, art deco mirrors, and original artwork.

A fed up girlfriend placed a rotating lawn sprinkler in the middle of the room, turned it on, and left it on for an entire weekend. To say the least, this wildly extravagant gesture put a damper on their relationship, not to mention ruining all his furnishings and compromising the foundation of his house.

FORE!

The world is full of golf widows, women dating or married to golfers who spend all of their free time hitting little white balls down empty green fairways. It's a compulsion that is incomprehensible to those who have never experienced golf's allure.

One day, Sara stopped by the golf course to surprise her golfing beau with an invitation for lunch. Imagine her astonishment when she saw him coaching a young woman golfer, his arms around her waist.

The next day, our avid golfer returned for his next session with his eager pupil. When he teed off, his golf ball exploded, showering him and his companion with a spray of black ink. Sara had replaced his balls (somehow it seemed appropriate) with the joke variety that explode on impact. (See Appendix for mail-order joke shops.)

LAWN GRAFFITI

Frieda's boyfriend purchased a house when their relationship was already in full swing. She soon realized it didn't bode well for their future as a couple. He loved the house and was fond of showing it off to his friends and colleagues. When he invited Frieda to move in as a roommate paying a high rent, she gave him his walking papers.

Her revenge was to deface his beautiful beloved lawn. She took a big bottle of bleach and burned a choice epithet into the grass. It's too X-rated to include here, but it was along the lines of 'A Dick Lives Here'.

An alternative for those with green thumbs would be to plant the message with grass that grows faster than regular grass. Or, if you're pressed for time, simply drive your car up on the lawn, gun your engine, and spin in fast circles.

PLASTIC UTENSILS
This offbeat story is a personal favourite. Oddly enough, it also targets the lawn. What is it about that expanse of green that brings out such destructive tendencies?

One woman purchased several hundred plastic forks, which she stuck in the ground tines up, all over the lawn. It was very cold that night and the ground froze. The next morning her ex, the man of the house, walked out barefoot to pick up his morning paper. He started across the grass as usual. Ouch! What's that picnic fork doing there? He reached down to pull it out. And guess what? It snapped leaving the handle still in the ground. Then he saw there were hundreds more of them all over the lawn, all impossible to pull out. He ended up having to plough the lawn under and start all over again.

ORAL HYGIENE
Okay, so this is a strange one, but it deserves applause for its twisted sense of humour. It also scores high on the originality scale, even though it would shock most mothers if they found out their daughters had resorted to such tactics. But, let's face it, people do odd

things when they're in the grip of rage.

Pat was getting ready for work in her boyfriend's bathroom. He'd already left for the office. The phone rang and without thinking she went to answer it. Imagine her surprise when the answering machine beat her to the punch and his ex-girlfriend (who didn't sound like an ex-girlfriend at all) was leaving a lovey-dovey message. The woman even had the cheek to make a reference to Pat and giggled, saying she hoped Pat was still in the dark about their secret romance.

Fuming, Pat grabbed the first thing she could find of his and threw it in the toilet. It just happened to be his toothbrush. Then she had a bizarre and wicked idea. She scrubbed away at the toilet with the toothbrush. Then she took a Polaroid of herself doing this menial cleaning job.

She put the toothbrush back in its holder and left. After that fateful morning, she refused to take her boyfriend's calls and swiftly changed her phone number.

After a couple of weeks had gone by, she posted the photo to him, knowing that he would have been using that toothbrush at least twice a day.

A GOOD SPORT Many women target their ex's sports-related toys. Why? Maybe it's because sports are often part of a domain that's strictly separate from a girlfriend.

One woman was dating a pro tennis player. After he abruptly ditched her to take up with a rich benefactor, the jilted woman snipped just one string on each and every one of his custom-made tennis racquets. This all occurred on the morning of one of his tournaments, so it was an act that definitely didn't go unnoticed.

Along the same lines, a young wife and mother of three children was married to a man who became a bowling fanatic. He would spend at least four nights a week at the local bowling alley. Even his wardrobe changed, and he took to wearing fifties-style bowling clothes all the time. Someone eventually tipped the wife off to the fact that her husband was spending a lot of time with one of the female members of his bowling team. One of the many things the wife did before filing for divorce was pack quick-drying wood putty into the holes of all his bowling balls.

MORE HOME REVENGE IDEAS

Call his voice mail and leave an entire episode of 'The Archers' on it.

Turn off his hot water.

Release a box of crickets in his home.

Turn all the clocks in his house back an hour.

Fill his vodka and gin bottles with water.

Put a can of sardines in the heating vent.

Hide his remote controls, especially the one in the bedroom.

Stash some raw eggs under the sofa cushions.

Carefully pour flour onto the blades of his ceiling fan – the next time he turns it on it'll be like Christmas. Or try pepper, ground coffee, maraschino cherries – whatever strikes your fancy.

Line up bars of chocolate on all the window ledges that are exposed to direct sunlight.

Draw soap designs on all his mesh screens. They're impossible to get off.

Fill an empty rubbish bin with water, lean it up against his door, ring the bell, then run like hell.

His Bedroom and Bathroom

Pour lots of pepper into his pillowcase.

Replace the K-Y jelly with Deep Heat.

Throw out all the toilet paper. Sounds petty, but it's annoying.

Fill his nasal spray with vinegar.

Replace his haemorrhoid cream with Vicks VapoRub.

Replace his Grecian Formula with transmission fluid.

Replace his hair spray with quick-drying wood varnish.

Put a beef bouillon cube in the shower head.

Mix jelly cubes with hot water and pour it into his toilet bowl. Let it set.

His Wardrobe

Cut the elastic waistbands in all his underwear.

Steal one shoe from each of his pairs.

Cut holes in the linings of all his pockets.

Pour honey in his shoes.

Cut all the buttons off his shirts.

Put itching powder in his socks.

Have all his clothes taken in.

Sprinkle bleach in his colourfast liquid detergent. Mixing in a nice pink dye might also be a hit.

Burn a big hole in the back of his tuxedo jacket. With any luck, he won't notice it.

Squirt lines of toothpaste into his suit jacket sleeves.

If he swims, cut a small hole in the rear panel of his swimming trunks. Hopefully he won't notice before going for a dip. It'll probably get bigger as he exerts himself.

Buy three dozen hungry moths and let them set up house in his wardrobe while he's on holiday.

His Toys

Cut several pages out of his favourite books.

Change the password on his computer.

Dull the edges of his skis.

Pack his video player with marshmallows.

Scratch all his favourite CDs and records.

Wreck his stamp collection by licking all the stamps and putting them in a book. This strips them of value.

His Garden

Cover the lawn with shredded newspaper, then douse it
   with water – picking it up will take days.

Install a skunk in his garden.

Sprinkle the lawn with antifreeze.

Bring thousands of aphids to live in his flower beds.

Call a contractor and arrange for his pool to be filled with
   concrete.

12
Fun With Tape and Glue

Tape and glue are God's gift to the woman avenger seeking swift yet effective revenge. They can be used to provide some annoying little surprises, to reconstruct his environment, even to destroy prized possessions.

PASS THE BOSTICK One irate sister spent a pleasant cathartic Saturday morning going around her ex-boyfriend's flat armed with glue and duct tape. First she went into the bathroom and glued the shower doors closed, glued all the cabinet doors closed, the toothbrush into its holder, the soap into its dish, and so forth.

In the kitchen she glued the fridge closed and all the cups to their kitchen shelf. Then she went around the entire flat gluing all the phones into their cradles and all the lightbulbs into their sockets. Before driving away, she packed glue into the keyhole in the front door and taped the letter box shut. In sum, she had a regular tape and glue fest.

Of course, you could get really carried away here and get into more costly acts of mischief, such as packing the CD player with glue, gluing the TV controls – you get the gist. It depends on how much wrath you feel can be purged by this kind of wanton destruction.

A WAKE-UP CALL

A female neighbour took this to another level. She did a double whammy, so to speak. She knew her boyfriend's morning routine well. A hard-core caffeine addict, he would always gulp down several cups of coffee as he showered and dressed.

She planned their last morning together carefully. She got up very early and gathered together all her possessions, happy knowing it was definitely time to leave this sorry excuse for a man behind. Before departing, she mixed a box of laxatives into the coffee grounds, and then – what inspiration! She glued the toilet seat shut. The result, no doubt, was particularly gruesome.

THE RELUCTANT GOURMET

Fiona's boyfriend was one of those people who had no imagination as far as food goes. She tried taking him to a variety of restaurants, but if he didn't find something familiar on the menu like hamburgers or spaghetti, he would simply order coffee and then sit looking in disgust at whatever she had ordered.

When he was at home, he maintained his culinary conservatism by eating mostly canned food. A lot of it was kid food, like canned ravioli, baked beans, tomato soup, and so forth.

One night Fiona invited him over for a home-cooked meal, and she made stuffed rock cornish game hens. Even though she told him they were basically just very small chickens, he refused to eat. He just pushed his bird around his plate like it was something that had been run over by a car. This was the last straw for Fiona. It was time to tell this neurotic twerp to take a hike. Before leaving him for good, she went to his flat armed with scissors and glue and switched all the labels on his canned food. You'd have to know this lunatic to grasp the impact this off-the-wall act would have. When he opened a can of corn and found it full of pineapple chunks, his world order was profoundly disturbed.

HAIR GLUE

Gerry, an old pal, told me about how she used glue revenge on one of her 'regrettables', as she calls boyfriends who turned out to be big disappointments. This guy was one of those mirror-glancers, always stopping to admire his hair at every opportunity.

Gerry was amazed at the amount of time this guy spent coiffing his hair. As she put it, if a guy has more products on his bathroom counter than you do, it's usually a bad sign. He worked on his 'do' much more than she did on hers. Before leaving for work in the morning, he would carefully blow-dry it, flicking it, rolling it, puffing it. Finally, he would spray it all over with hair spray.

Gerry knew the cardinal revenge rule, which is to target your mark's most vulnerable area. She emptied out his can of hair spray and replaced it with a light liquid glue. That final day, she watched him go through his preening routine, ending with the usual all-over spray. He raced out the door and rushed to work. It wasn't until he was in his office that he glanced in a mirror and noticed that his hair was as stiff as a board. The poor vain creature had to suffer the entire day before he could go home and wash the glue out, which, when he finally did, was no easy task.

WHERE'S MY DOOR?

Now this is a weird one – how about making his front door disappear altogether? This was a ploy devised by a female contractor, a woman who used her skills to get back at a louse in her life. She sealed the perimeter of his front door with plaster and then stuccoed over it. Imagine him coming home to find the front door gone. There was just a blank wall. Talk about surreal.

SUPER GLUE
Super Glue is by far the most extreme of all weapons of adhesion. Revenge acts involving Super Glue are nuclear weapons, especially if they involve the human body. Super Glue can only be removed from human skin through medical intervention, usually involving an embarrassing trip to casualty. Save acts involving Super Glue for the most diabolical situations.

A few years ago a woman in Chicago had reached her limit with a husband who'd been unfaithful to her over and over again. Every time she found out about yet another affair, he pleaded for another chance and promised it would never happen again. But, of course, it did. Finally, tired of his empty promises, she took matters into her own hands and rendered him true to his word – at least for a while: She glued his penis to his abdomen while he slept.

Another woman went beyond that obvious little appendage. She glued her philandering husband's hands together while he slept, and then left the house. Imagine his surprise on waking up. How could he drive himself to casualty to get unstuck? And how could he make a phone call to get help? The ramifications are endless. Oh, to be a fly on the wall in that 'sticky' situation.

13
His Hallowed Office

Embarrassing your ex at work can be particularly effective, as the work-place is usually an arena where men present a carefully controlled picture of themselves. Having his dirty laundry exposed to his colleagues will really rattle his cage and deflate his bloated self-image.

SO LONG, DOC Alexis had dated her paediatrician boyfriend for two years. She broke up with him when she found out he'd been two-timing her with an anaesthesiologist. Alexis racked her brain to figure out how to get back at him and came up with a nifty little plan. She went to his office early one morning and buried a few sex magazines in the piles of reading materials in the waiting room. To add authenticity, she carefully removed his address labels from magazines like *National Geographic* and *Highlights* and glued them onto the X-rated covers.

E-MAIL REVENGE Jeanine knew that her ex, a stockbroker, loved getting e-mail. He always checked it first thing in the morning when he sat down at his desk.

Jeanine also knew that he worked in close quarters with many other colleagues. There were forty or so stockbrokers packed into one huge room. So when she signed him up on-line for partner-swapping and sex games, and even plugged him into a bestiality network, Jeanine knew that it would be impossible for him to hide all the saucy messages that came up on his computer all day long.

THANK-YOU GIFT
Skip this one if you're squeamish. Isabel lives in northern California, an area famous for, among other things, huge slimy yellow slugs called banana slugs. To get back at her ex (who was also her boss), she went into the forest and collected a bunch of these slugs. Then – gasp – she processed them in a blender. (Slug rights activists, please don't write and complain.)

Isabel poured the result into one of those pretty old-fashioned jam jars. She sealed it, labelled it 'Banana Jam', and tied it with a nice yellow ribbon. She then left it on her ex's desk with a note thanking him for being such a great boss.

JUMBO E-MAIL
Lisa and Jake used to send each other e-mail almost every morning. It was a nice way to start off the workday. Once their relationship took a dive, Lisa vented her anger by sending jumbo e-mails with intricate graphics that take half an hour to download.

Watching e-mail download is as tedious as watching paint dry. And if fast e-mail communication is intrinsic to his work, especially first thing in the morning, this can be a very effective downer. On many computers, once these files start downloading, there's no way to stop them.

Jake soon caught on and stopped opening e-mails from Lisa. But that didn't stop her. She started sending them in the evening from computers all over town – in libraries and copy shops. Okay, so she got a little nutty for a while, but some of the most stable people get crazy from time to time.

CONSUMER COMPLAINTS The Internet is a great new world that opens up new ways of communicating. It's also a powerful revenge tool. Not only does it offer a cornucopia of revenge supplies and services (see Appendix), it provides other opportunities for the avenger. For example, you might capitalize on the Internet's usefulness as a forum where consumers can warn each other about frauds and scam artists.

A nuclear attack on him might be to post a consumer complaint targeting his company. Again, be sure to temper your revenge, because you can do serious damage to a person's business or reputation.

Imagine, for example, that he owns a carpet cleaning company. You can post an angry complaint that his company damaged your carpets, broke a priceless vase, trashed your sofa – whatever makes him look bad.

This is a powerful tactic, so use it with care – and don't open yourself to a lawsuit.

JELLY REVENGE Once Diana found out about her husband's infidelity, she embarked on a series of revenge acts before suing him for divorce. One evening she watched as her husband wrote a proposal to present to an important new client the next morning. He then slipped the proposal into his briefcase.

After he'd gone to sleep, Diana made a huge bowl of strawberry jelly and emptied it into the briefcase. The next day her husband began his presentation, reached into his briefcase for the proposal, and pulled out a handful of goo.

The client was less than impressed.

Other variations on this theme might be to fill the briefcase with shaving cream, sand, or even concrete.

BACK TO BASICS
Most men think they are wonderful lovers. Of course, only their women know for sure. You might consider sending your ex a copy of *The Better Sex* video. Include a note, such as, 'Isn't it about time you learned your ABCs?'

MYSTERIOUS AROMAS
Suzanna's ex-husband, a personal injury lawyer, had an impressive office on the fifteenth floor of a high-rise building. Focusing on the office for a revenge plot seemed like the correct karma for Mr. Bigshot. One afternoon Suzanna slipped into her ex-hubby's office, peeled the lid off a can of gourmet cat food, and hid it discreetly behind a filing cabinet. It wasn't long before that spectacular office was transformed into a stinky hell hole.

EX-FILES
It's a fact of life that many accountants are, by nature, obsessive compulsives. Deidre soon found out that her accountant boyfriend was insanely preoccupied with meticulous order. He was particularly proud of his impeccably neat filing system.

Their relationship ended on Valentine's Day, when he invited Deidre over for a romantic meal at his home and then, as usual, spent the entire evening working. Deidre waited until he was asleep, and then went through his file cabinets leaving choice messages like 'Dick' under D, 'Shithead' under S – you get the drift.

MR. HOMOPHOBIC

In retrospect, there were many signs that Lilian's partner had some unhealthy attitudes. When they drove through the area of town that was predominantly gay, he would pretend to shoot the male couples with an invisible machine-gun. One day when they were stuck in traffic waiting to let a gay pride parade pass by, he made a dark comment about the need to legalize euthanasia.

After their nasty break-up, he hysterically accused Lilian of being unnaturally intimate with one of her female friends. She decided she had to target his bigotry in her revenge.

Lilian had a beautiful gift basket delivered to him at work. In it were some male homosexual magazines, K-Y jelly, a penis-shaped lollipop, and other speciality items. For an extra flourish, she included a card: 'See you Friday night. Love, James.'

LIMP LINGUINE

Doris had made the cardinal error of having a fling with one of her work colleagues. It was a tricky situation that might have been handled well if two mature adults were involved. However, like many men, this fellow took the coward's way out and gave her the cold shoulder as if nothing had ever happened.

Doris decided a nice little goodbye gift was in order. She came to work early one morning and left on his desk, for all to see, a strand of limp linguine. On a card she wrote in big bold letters: 'Don't worry too much. It happens to all men at one time or another.'

LOVE ON THE RUN

Sherry worked as a dispatcher for a taxi cab company, where she had been dating one of the mechanics for five years. Suddenly, out of the blue, he dumped her, offering no real explanation. He said he just wanted to be single.

The next morning she made him a cup of hot chocolate and took it out to him in the service area. She handed it over with a smile. He was pleased that she was taking the break-up so well. What he didn't know was that she had dumped a box of laxatives into his drink. He spent the rest of the day running back and forth to the toilet. And that smile never left her face.

14
His Pets

It goes without saying that you should never ever harm animals in your quest for revenge on a human, but there are a few ways you can get the little critters to work with you in getting back at your ex.

TINY PAW PRINTS
Alice's boyfriend had one of those annoying tiny terriers that scamper everywhere at high speed yapping their little heads off. Before bidding her boyfriend adieu, she dipped the little darling's paws in ink and left him to scamper all over her beloved's home.

I LOVE MY DOG
It's galling when your boyfriend or mate displays more affection for his pet than he does for you, his lover. How many of us have watched our significant others shower their kitty or pooch with kisses or compliments in a sweet high-pitched voice they never use when talking to us?

Alison had had it with her beau's obsession with his female malamute. He idolized the dog, worshipping her like a fur-covered goddess. Alison came to hate the dog, which got all the love and attention denied her. (Her boyfriend never ever rolled Alison over, rubbed her belly, and murmured sweet nothings, yet he'd spend hours caressing the dog in such a fashion.) The worst part was that he let the dog sleep on the bed, even when Alison was sleeping over.

The last morning she slept there, Alison looked over and saw the boyfriend and the dog lying together, the dog's head on the pillow next to him, its paws flung casually across his chest. Alison realized it was time to do something radical. Being a good avenger, she knew she had to hit him where it would hurt the most.

Her boyfriend was preparing the dog for breeding. He was trying to find a worthy mate, one with excellent malamute lineage. When he spoke of this, his voice cracked and tears almost welled in his eyes. He told her he looked forward to keeping one of the pets. Jesus! Two dogs for him to fawn over.

Alison decided to hold off her big sayonara until the malamute was next in heat. She went to her guy's house, picked up the dog, and drove it to a seedy part of town. There she scoured the alleys and sought out the ugliest mutt she could find. She pushed the bitch out of the car and watched as the mutt casually impregnated her.

Alison brought the malamute back home and left a note saying: 'So long, sucker!' She decided not to spill the beans on what she'd done. After all, Nature would soon show herself in all her wonder and glory.

DOG LOVER

Denise was aware that her boyfriend went every afternoon to his local dog club, one of those popular groups of dogs and owners that meet daily in American city parks usually in the late afternoon. Denise didn't think much about it until one day she happened to drive by the park and saw her boyfriend sniffing all over an attractive young Rotweiler owner.

Denise came up with a wonderfully creative revenge scheme. She sprayed a fine mist of dog urine on his trouser legs. There wasn't enough for a human nose to detect, but more than enough to attract the finely tuned canine nose. The next day, when Romeo went to the park, all the dogs went nuts. Dog after dog peed on his trouser legs. Yes, all in front of the young woman and her Rotweiler. Romeo was thoroughly humiliated. Denise gleefully hid in a nearby bush, stifling her laughter as she snapped photographs to commemorate the occasion.

A MAKEOVER There are a number of stories in which ex-girlfriends give their boyfriend's beloved dogs free makeovers. One girlfriend treated her ex's giant poodle to a session with a clipper who gave the dog a froufrou French poodle look. This was embarrassing for the dog's owner, because he was an uptight jock type who hated the cat calls and horn honkings that he elicited when he walked the dog in the neighbourhood.

15
Public Humiliations

Public humiliations can be very effective. Remember America's Anita Hill and Clarence Thomas, a spectacle labelled by Ms. Hill's detractors as a bitter woman's revenge? Anita Hill, in fact, did not instigate this distorted public airing of dirty laundry, that revealed problems way beyond Clarence Thomas's weird behaviour. As Eleanor Smeal, president of the Fund for the Feminist Majority commented, 'The Senate did more in one week to underscore the critical need for more women in the Senate than feminists have been able to do in twenty-five years.'

Of course, none of us can expect this kind of public forum to air the wrongdoings of our men, but there are other ways to publicly humiliate them on a smaller scale.

MOTORWAY SIGNS Poor Kelly contracted V.D. from her wayward boyfriend. Talk about a double punch. Infidelity plus disease!

She defused her anger with one grand public humiliation. Early one morning she snuck onto an overpass on the very busy motorway the jerk used to drive to work and hung a sign alerting the public to her ex's positive V.D. test.

Naturally, she didn't hang around to be arrested for this public advertisement. But she relished the thought of literally thousands of drivers learning her ex's dirty little secret.

THE INTERNET A site on the Internet for avengers is
ExLovers.com where you can actually post nude photographs of and horror stories about your ex for all the world to view. There are actually five sites: Ex-Wives, Ex-Husbands, Ex-Lovers, Ex-Girlfriends, and Ex-Boyfriends.

According to the front page, these sites are 'dedicated to all of us individuals who have been screwed over by our exes. . . . Just when they thought they had the last word, the Internet comes along. . . . They got the gold mine and we got the shaft!'

Membership to these sites also allows access to practical information on how to be your own detective, high-tech surveillance devices for adulterous spouses, divorce and child support laws, and more.

Another good site is Lover's Revenge, a cyber carnival game where you can lob water balloons at moving human targets, which you pretend are your ex. As you score points, you win back your CDs, books, letters, and other items still in his possession. (See Appendix for more information on these sites and others.)

A JUICY BESTSELLER A tell-all book like the one
Mia Farrow wrote about her long relationships with Woody Allen and others is a nice form of catharsis. Tell-all books also allow you to rag on about your mark without him or her being able to respond. And, you make money in the process. On the downside, of course, you or your ex should be a celebrity, or nobody will really care.

HI, I'M NOT HOME . . .

You might be tempted to change the message on his phone answering machine. Most of these machines have a three-digit code, which isn't hard to crack, especially since many people select obvious combinations of numbers. Enlist a male pal to provide the voice for authority.

You could also publicly embarrass your ex by recording a nice friendly message on his office machine: 'Hi, I'm out for a liquid lunch, but leave me a message and I'll call you back when I feel like it.' If he's a doctor, you might try: 'Hi, this is Dr. X's office. I'm sorry but we're closed due to a malpractice suit.' And at home: 'Hi, this is the X residence. We can't come to the phone right now 'cause we're having our hot gay orgy night. Come by if you want to join in.'

BREAKFAST TELEVISION

Jillian came up with an interesting public humiliation to get back at her exboyfriend, Fritz, a handsome and conceited guy who had been carrying on a long-term affair with a married girlfriend simultaneously with his relationship with Jillian. Somehow, the fact that the girlfriend was married made him feel like it didn't count as full-blown infidelity. He dismissed it as an occasional diversion. 'It doesn't mean anything,' he explained. 'We just enjoy having sex with each other, that's all.' Yikes!

Knowing that Fritz usually watched America's *The Today Show* as he got ready for work each day, Jillian planted herself in the New York crowd that hovers outside the set every weekday morning. She held a big placard with the words: 'I Love You, Matt' and wore a silly Dr. Seuss hat so that she would stand out even more. She waited until the outdoor camera panned the crowd and lingered on her. Then she flipped the sign. On the back for all the world to

11

see were the words: 'Fritz is a Worthless Shit.' Actually, I felt she was quite restrained in her choice of epithets.

STUD SERVICES
Gloria's boyfriend lived in one of those sprawling Los Angeles apartment complexes with palm trees and a big swimming pool. She knew he was proud of his somewhat average body and loved to hang out by the pool, wearing those small swimming suits that most men should relegate permanently to the back of the bottom drawer.

After finding out he'd been 'seeing' one of the airline stewardesses who lived in a neighbouring apartment, Gloria decided a public humiliation was definitely the ticket for this schlub.

She found an X-rated picture of a nude male, pasted her boyfriend's head on it, and hung it in the laundry room at his apartment complex. She wrote on it with a black marker: 'Stud Services Available. Apartment 18.'

Since she was well aware that he hated doing laundry and let it accumulate for weeks at a time, she knew the picture would be there for quite some time before he discovered it.

Since he was clearly a neanderthal, she probably would have been well within her rights to post something even more incendiary like: 'Herpes Alert! Apartment 18.'

FAKE CREDENTIALS
Remember how he once confided to you that he had faked information on his CV? If he's really done a number on you, you might consider exposing him. Be careful, however. You don't want to appear like a malicious shrew. Think of a creative way to do it that doesn't implicate you. For example, you might send a letter to his boss from 'an old ex-employer' stating

that questions are being raised about the legitimacy of your ex's credentials and asking for assistance. Then sit back and let events unfold. This should at least trigger some very probing questions at his office.

I WANT TO THANK . . . Cara and her boyfriend

were together all through film school. They struggled through those tough years living on very little money. Finally, her boyfriend got his big break. A short film he made won a prize at one of the major film festivals.

Cara noticed her boyfriend suddenly had very little time for her. He was constantly going out for business lunches and dinners to which she was not invited. After he told her he didn't have room for a personal relationship anymore and that he had to concentrate on his career, she decided this guy needed to be cut down to size.

She knew that he was soon going to receive an award from a group of film critics, so she called him up and offered in a very friendly way to pick up his rented tuxedo. Mr. Big Head actually agreed to let her take on this menial role in his life. Cara delivered the tuxedo and stuck around. While he took a shower, she sprinkled itching powder into his new Calvin Klein underwear.

He didn't notice the discomfort until he was already in the limo on his way to the event. By the time he had to give his speech, he was in agony and kept grabbing at himself in a most undignified manner.

16
Unwanted Suitors

Unwanted suitors can rear their ugly heads in a number of ways. There are the ones you know, like the jerk in the office who thinks he's God's gift to women and who harasses you at every opportunity or the bore you had one date with who keeps calling, despite countless rejections. And then there are the ones you don't know, like the perennial obscene phone callers or the builders who bellow from their high perches like mindless chimps.

HEAVY BREATHERS This is an old trick that always works in getting rid of those morons with nothing better to do with their time than call complete strangers, breathe heavily, and mutter obscenities.

Keep a whistle next to the phone. Next time the idiot calls, talk softly for a few moments so he cups the phone really close to his ear. When you have his full attention, blast him!

Alternatively, you can use the feature available on many phones that will automatically call back the number of the last incoming call. Adopt a polite phone voice and say something like, 'Hello, I'm calling from your local phone company. I'd like to inform you that we are passing on to the police a complaint that obscene phone calls are being made from your phone number.' This should shut the slimeball up permanently.

One friend took a completely different, though highly effective, tack. She'd been bothered several times over by an obscene phone caller. Instead of freaking out and slamming the phone down, she started talking to him like he was an old friend: 'Oh, hi. How are you doing? You'll never guess what happened to me at the office today . . .' He was so surprised that he hung up and never called back. This is the kind of psychological defence akin to the streetwise tip that you throw a mugger off balance by simply laughing out loud in his face. In other words, do the opposite of what is expected in a given situation, and never show fear or intimidation.

FREEWAY FLASHERS This is a little-documented phenomenon, but several years ago, when women in L.A. first started driving four-wheel drive vehicles that are typically higher off the ground than your regular sedan, a horde of freeway flashers came creeping out of the woodwork. This happened to me – not once but twice – and I have two other friends who experienced this same weird kind of unwanted attention.

The scenario goes like this. A woman's driving along in her sport utility vehicle when she becomes aware that the car in the next lane is speeding up and slowing down, trying to stay alongside her. The thought of freeway shootings flashes across her mind. She glances over, only to discover the weapon the man is armed with is his penis, which he is pumping vigorously as he hurtles along at 70 miles per hour, getting off on the fact that the woman in the next vehicle has a full view of his genitals.

In one of my encounters, the offender was one of those

freaks you hear about with an unnaturally large appendage. It's a sight that would make most women blanche, realizing that an attack by this pervert would not be a rape but an assault with a deadly weapon.

At the time of this freeway flasher epidemic, few of us had mobile phones with which to call for help. (What would we say anyway? Would the 911 operator agree that being pursued by a twelve-inch penis hurtling along at 70 mph was a legitimate emergency?) This is a time when you should *not* seek revenge. Forget about personal revenge plots when you're dealing with real wackos. Just turn the other way. I floored it and tried to lose him by changing freeways. It took twenty nerve-wracking sweaty miles to finally ditch him.

THE CUCUMBER Here's another tale from the fun-filled trenches of modern urban life. Margie was in the vegetable section of a supermarket. She is an open, friendly person, so when a young man came up to her and asked her for help in buying a cucumber, she willingly complied.

'You have to look for a nice deep colour,' she said, picking a nice specimen out of the pile. 'The trick is to squeeze it like this. You don't want one that's all soft and squishy.'

At this point she glanced at the guy, who had this sick and twisted grin on his face and his eyes were kind of glazed and starting to roll up in his head. She realized she'd just been violated – at least in his warped little brain.

Physical violence is not something to be condoned. Let's face it, it can land you in court, and if you're not a rich celebrity, chances are you'll pay a stiff price. But in this case, Margie did what any self-respecting person would applaud. She took the cucumber and bashed him over the head with it. As the shop employees converged on the scene, the pervert hightailed it out the door.

THE OFFICE JERK
If you're being harassed at work, do not hesitate to take full advantage of the laws surrounding sexual harassment. But, if like many of us, you prefer to steer clear of red tape and officialdom, and if you live in the U.S., consider hiring Rent-a-Kvetch. For fees ranging from $50 to $100, Rent-a-Kvetch will harass the person who wronged you and will ensure your complaint gets heard by the right people. (See Appendix.)

Another way to go is to just fire your own little missile into the creep's world. For example, put a nicely wrapped gift under the office Christmas tree with his name on it. Sign it: 'Love, Gavin.' Have it be some raunchy sex toy.

MORE OFFICE JERKS
When tackling the office Romeo, some women choose to fight fire with fire. A group of women in a Manchester telemarketing firm had had their fill of a male employee who flitted amongst them like some sex-crazed honeybee. They fought back at this pest by faxing a very embarrassing erotic note to the fax machine he shared with several colleagues. The note was carefully worded and alluded to his unusual sexual tastes, involving small furry animals and parts of his anatomy that have never been exposed to direct sunlight.

A variation of this would be to leave a note from the jerk to some good looking male employee in the office photo-copying machine. Or compose a propositioning love note signed by him and address it to the boss's secretary. Place the note in the boss's pigeon hole. Just keep in mind that you might also hurt an innocent party.

THE NUDE VET
Diane is a technical writer who specializes in producing promotional materials for animal

feed companies. One summer she landed a nice contract with a major dog food company that required her to write a series of informational booklets for vets, outlining the value of the company's products to dogs' health.

Diane's contact person at the company was a suave, well-coiffed ex-vet who was hired to travel the country promoting the dog food through local radio appearances and so forth. Although Diane and the vet lived in different cities, they developed a decent working relationship over the phone, as he helped her translate the scientific material into everyday language.

One day he called out of the blue to say he'd be in her city for a day, and asked her to meet him for a working dinner. Since he was not familiar with the restaurants in the area, they arranged that Diane would pick him up at his hotel.

When she knocked on his door, he greeted her wearing nothing but his birthday suit. You can hardly give a swift kick to the balls of the man responsible for your pay cheque. Or can you? Since he'd already crossed the line into another zone of interaction, couldn't she?

Being a cool chick, Diane quickly assessed the situation and, quelling her desire to laugh out loud, she instead completely ignored the fact that he was nude. She looked him straight in the eyes and without a flinch said, 'I see you're not quite ready. I'll wait for you in the car.'

Dumbstruck, he watched her walk down the corridor. Her response nicely pricked (Freudian slip) his self-image. If he expected the sight of his naked body would cause her to fall into a passionate swoon, he certainly got a rude awakening.

They went on to have their dinner, never again speaking of the incident. Their relationship remained strictly business from that point on.

17
Voodoo

Voodoo means 'to bewitch'. In traditional voodoo cere-
monies, people went into frenzied trances in which they
become possessed by the Loa, or one of the hundreds of
voodoo gods. Since love affairs can drive us to feel possessed
and under the influence of powerful forces, it's not surprising that some might resort to voodoo to exorcise the root
cause of their captivation.

Depending on how superstitious you are, you may not
want to dabble in voodoo at all. Who knows what you might
conjure up? But if you do want to go the voodoo route, read
on for some easy schemes and recipes based on mysterious
rituals and ancient magic. (You will also find suggestions for
additional reading material in the Appendix.)

VOODOO DOLLS
Voodoo dolls are the most familiar
voodoo symbols. Sticking a doll with pins can be a potent
ritual of exorcism, giving us a sense of real or imagined
power over our target.

One popular voodoo doll available in joke shops is a
little stuffed figure that comes equipped with black and
white pins. This doll is labelled with positive and negative

wishes. The white pins might be stuck into positives such as 'happiness', 'win in Vegas', 'kittens' and 'no back pain' while the black pins get stuck into off-the-wall curses such as 'lose hair', 'lose mind', 'slugs' and 'weeds'.

VIRTUAL VOODOO DOLL
You can access a virtual voodoo doll on the Web. (This is an interesting and eclectic blend of an ancient practice with modern technology.) Just bring the doll up on your screen and torture it using needles, candles, and knives. You can then e-mail it to your ex.

Your ex will receive the e-mail with a URL, which will take him directly to the web site. There, he'll be treated to a graphic animated replay of the abuse, complete with tribal drums and screams of pain. (For more information on this terrific resource, see the Appendix.)

HOMEMADE VOODOO DOLLS
The most authentic doll is one you make yourself. The easiest way is to use a small rock, nut, or apple for the head, drape a piece of sacking or cloth over it, and then bind it with a piece of twine around the neck.

An old voodoo practice is to fashion a doll out of corn husks and then bury it under the floorboards of your mark's house. This will bring evil and bad luck upon him. Of course, if your boyfriend has a parquet floor or wall-to-wall carpeting, this might be hard to pull off.

How to Torture Your Voodoo Doll
Stick it with pins.
Run it over with your car.
Tie it to the bumper of your car, and go for a fast drive on the motorway.

Douse it with petrol and set it on fire.

Toss it down a public portable toilet, preferably at an event with a big crowd.

Cut it in half with a saw.

Drill holes into it.

Drown it.

Tie it to a bottle rocket and launch it into space.

Rub it down with bacon and toss it to a pit bull.

Leave it on a horse-trekking trail to be pounded by many hooves.

Skewer it and roast it over a fire, cannibal style.

Squash it in a hydraulic press.

Grind it up with a lawnmower.

Pull a plastic bag over its head and suffocate it.

Toss it into a raging incinerator.

Push it down a storm drain.

Whip it till its skin shreds off.

Tar and feather it.

Tie a rope around its neck and bash it against a brick wall.

Take it to a building site and toss it into a vat of molten concrete.

Throw it off a high cliff, one with jagged rocks below to 'break' its fall.

Sprinkle it with acid, then watch it slowly burn.

Stick a hot poker into its eye sockets.

Toss it into a boat propeller.

Pretend it's a French aristocrat and guillotine it.

Using Voodoo to Exorcise His Evil Presence

Ancient voodoo priests used their powers to combat evil spirits and bad luck. If your recent romance falls into those categories, consider an easy voodoo spell you can perform in the privacy of your own home. All you'll need is a fresh brown egg, a brown paper bag, and a piece of black string.

Make sure the moon is waning on the night before you

begin the spell. Purchase the fresh brown egg before midday. Place the egg in a brown paper bag and tie the neck of the bag with the black string.

Before you go to bed, open the bag, take out the egg, and rub it all over your body. Put the egg back in the bag, then blow into the bag three times. Imagine that with each breath the evil influences and bad luck are leaving your body. Then place the bag under your bed while you sleep.

Do this for nine days in a row. Then dispose of the egg and the bag somewhere far away from your home.

A word of caution: always tie up the bag immediately after you expel air into it. If after seven days you notice that the bag is moving on its own, stop the spell immediately and make haste to dispose of the bag. *Do not look inside*.

Revenge Powder

Revenge powder is something you can make up in the privacy of your own home and then scatter around your domicile to protect you from the evil one. Most of the ingredients are available in supermarkets:

2 tablespoons garlic powder
1 teaspoon mustard
1 teaspoon paprika
1 teaspoon sage
3 drops human blood

Put all the ingredients in a small bowl made of wood or another natural substance. Mix them with a twig while muttering something sinister like 'May he be covered in warts', 'let toads rain down on him' or 'make that new Mazda of his be sideswiped in a car park'. Sprinkle pinches of the powder around the perimeter of your home to stop the evil one from entering (unless of course he's begging for forgiveness and is bearing expensive gifts, in which case you should grab the loot, then slam the door in his face).

Voodoo Supplies
There are voodoo shops in America that offer a whole range of revenge supplies and there's also a web site that offers mail-order voodoo specifically for revenge situations. (See the Appendix for information on all these resources.)

18
What If He's Married?

Now this is a touchy subject, especially if you believe in sisterhood and all that. But chances are you knew he was married before you got into it with him, right? So aren't you also responsible for breaking the commandment, 'Thou shalt not commit adultery'?

Many of us may have dallied with another woman's man at one time or another, but the most important thing to adhere to after an unpleasant break-up with a married man is not to take it out on his wife. It's just not fair. You've already been dipping your bucket in her well, so to speak. Don't add insult to injury by punishing her for his sins. Keep your revenge sights firmly trained where they should be: on him.

MILLION-DOLLAR REVENGE In a recent landmark American court case, a scorned wife sued 'the other woman' for alienation of affection. It didn't help when the other woman came to court dressed in dowdy clothes, looking like Granny in *The Beverly Hillbillies*. The resourceful wife responded by producing photographs of what the real vixen was like – dressed to the nines in a tight

little Joan Collins business suit. The jury unanimously sided with the wife and directed the new honey to cough up an astounding $1 million! That certainly put a dent in her plans to set up house with her lover.

A MINOR OMISSION It's astounding to hear of the number of women who have been romanced by men who hide the fact that they are married as if it's just some minor detail in their lives.

Sylvia met a wonderful man as she was riding up the glass lift of a big hotel. After admiring the spectacular views together, they lingered to chat in the corridor. When he invited her to meet him for dinner that night, she happily accepted.

After spending most of the next two days with him, she felt that she had truly fallen in love. While they were in bed in his room on their last night together, the phone rang. Sylvia could hear the woman's voice on the other end. She was startled as she heard him also talk to a young child. He was very casual about the whole thing. When he hung up, she asked him in a quivering voice who he had been talking to. When he offhandedly replied, 'my wife', she realized she'd been horribly deceived. She angrily got out of bed and pulled on her clothes. He laughed and said she was taking it way too seriously. It was only a couple of days of fun. What was she expecting? A proposal of marriage? She realized that he was a sleep-around and probably made a habit of these fleeting hotel romances.

Sylvia immediately walked out on this cad. Back in her room, she fumed with humiliation. It was galling how relaxed he'd remained throughout their encounter. She wondered how she might retaliate. An idea came to her.

Sylvia used her mobile phone to call hotel security. She reported that a hotel guest had just stepped out of his room and exposed himself to her. She gave lover-boy's room number and hung up without leaving her name. She then packed her suitcase and while she was checking out, she angrily complained that a man had just exposed himself to her in the lift. She described lover-boy to a tee, right down to the mole on his you-know-what. Saying she was late for a business meeting, she turned on her heel and left the hotel feeling vindicated.

CHOCOLATE REVENGE
In Margaret Atwood's short story 'Hairball', a jilted mistress sends her ex and his wife an elegant box, which she knows they will open at a lavish party they are throwing. Inside the box in a bed of shredded tissue paper the woman had placed a large tumour which her doctors had just removed from her ovaries. She nestled some two dozen chocolate truffles around the tumour, then carefully wrapped the box with pink tissue paper and tied it with a mauve bow. In her mind, the tumour was the only child she and this man would ever have, and she wanted to shock the couple who started their relationship while he was still tied to the mistress. Call me old-fashioned, but I would draw the line at anything that involves blood or body parts.

THE SECRETARY
In John Cheever's short story, 'The Five-Forty-Eight', a secretary takes revenge on her boss. She is a waiflike young woman who works for a middle-class family man who spends weekdays in the city and weekends at home in Connecticut with his wife and children.

The man cruelly takes advantage of the young woman's neediness when they embark on an affair. When he's done with her, he drops her with little regard for her sincere attachment to him. The woman is left to mope by herself while the jerk goes back to his comfortable life.

One day the woman quietly boards the commuter train on which the boss travels home from the city. To his surprise, she sits down opposite him and reveals a gun that she has concealed beneath her coat. When the train stops at a station, she orders him to disembark. She marches him into a field and makes him kneel down in the mud. He cries, convinced she's about to execute him. To his surprise, she turns around and walks away, her mission accomplished. With this stunt, the woman was able to reverse the imbalance of power between them. He got his comeuppance and she got control.

HIS SHRINK WIFE There's an intriguing Berg-manesque story about a woman, Delia, whose lover was married to a lady shrink. When Delia and her lover broke up, it killed her to think of him back in his wife's arms, while she would once again be spending every night alone. After lying around night after night deep in the doldrums, she began to formulate a poisonous plan.

She carefully orchestrated her revenge to shatter her lover's marriage. Delia began seeing the shrink/wife as a patient. Over time, Delia revealed to the shrink that she was having an affair with a married man. In each session that followed she revealed yet another piece of incriminating evidence. The sequence of revelation went something like this:

Session 1: 'I'm having an affair with someone who's married.'

Session 2: 'He's six feet tall, has brown eyes, and smokes cigars.' The shrink doesn't make the connection. The description's still pretty vague.

Session 3: 'He drives a black Porsche.' 'Like my husband,'
    thinks the shrink.
Session 4: 'His wife's a shrink. I wonder if you know her.'

And so on, and so on. It's called sticking in the knife and
then slowly twisting it. You can imagine what was going on
in the shrink's mind as she started to put the pieces of Delia's
jigsaw puzzle together.

 Now, this is really not a very nice story. I mean, is it the
poor shrink's fault she's married to this two-timer? Whatever
you do, be careful not to take it out on an innocent victim.
It's almost as if this was just Delia's covert plan to get rid of
the lover's wife. And that's no way to win a guy.

19
His New Girlfriend

So he has a new girlfriend. You've been replaced. Grrr. This is really hard to swallow. Not only has he screwed you over, now he's rolling around in kissy city with a whole new babe. And murder, unfortunately, is still illegal.

Now remember, it's not good form to take out your revenge on *her*. After all, like the unsuspecting wife, the new girlfriend is usually an innocent third party. Remember how you felt when you first met him? It takes a while for the schmuck to reveal how cheap and sleazy he really is. Kind of like those cute little dinosaurs in *Jurassic Park*. How was the poor slob with the glasses to know they were about to spit blinding acid into his eyes, stomp him in the mud, and eat him for lunch? At least you got out alive. But that poor new girlfriend has no idea what's waiting for her down the road, because one thing's for sure – guys like him repeat the same tawdry dance over and over. Only the partners change.

So leave her alone. She is an innocent soon-to-be victim. And who knows? Down the road you may end up meeting with her to drink margaritas and swap stories about the jerk. Some women really do end up being friends after going through the same experience with the same heel. It's kind of like the camaraderie that springs up between people who work in the same office. And most men hate it when their girlfriends get together and gossip about them. Talk about the ultimate lack of control.

However (and this is the good part), there are exceptions. If she was once a friend who stole your man in cold blood, then she's well deserving of your revenge. After all, this is a double dumping. You were dumped by him *and* you were dumped by her. Very dirty business.

In this situation, there are a number of juicy little acts of revenge that you can resort to without any pangs of conscience. Hopefully they'll help to smooth your ruffled feathers.

V.D. ALERT
Pam's ex lost no time getting a new girlfriend. In fact, within days of their break-up he was out winning over his next conquest – and Pam hadn't even had the time to clear her belongings out of his flat.

Pam called his answering machine and left a message saying she'd like to pick up her stuff sometime during the next weekend. He called back and very generously offered to let her come and collect it on Saturday morning when he'd be out playing squash.

She tried not to notice the new pink toothbrush that was already installed in the bathroom. She avoided looking into the bedroom, where there was a lace camisole hanging on the big handsome sleigh bed, the one she'd helped him to pick out. But what she did do was leave an open letter where the new girlfriend would be most likely to find it. The letter was a confirmation of his next appointment at a venereal disease clinic.

Pam found some consolation in knowing that even if the boyfriend denied it, chances are his new girlfriend, if she had any smarts at all, would demand proof of a clean bill of health before getting naked. And for Pam, it made being alone the next weekend all the more easy to handle.

LUCY'S REVENGE

Lucy still had her ex-boyfriend's key. He'd been so busy revelling in his new love interest that it had slipped his mind. One lunch hour Lucy went over to his house. She knew her ex was very particular about having separate bathrooms. So she zeroed in on the guest bathroom, knowing it would be the exclusive domain of the new squeeze.

First, she stocked the bathroom cabinet with a selection of crass neon condoms. Then she placed *A Man's Guide to Rough Sex* (any hard-core porno magazine will do) next to the toilet. And for the pièce de résistance, so to speak, she hung a big dildo, the kind that comes with a mean-looking leather belt, over the taps in the guest shower.

THE BIKINI

To her annoyance, Amanda heard that her ex was going to Hawaii with his new girlfriend. To make matters worse, this was a trip he'd always been too busy to make during his relationship with her. Without breaking the law, Amanda managed to get into the new girlfriend's flat: her rival lived on the ground floor and often left her balcony door open.

Amanda rifled through her clothes and found a new bikini she'd purchased for the trip. Fortunately, the receipt was still in the bag. Amanda immediately drove to the department store and exchanged the bikini for one that was two sizes smaller, then returned to the apartment and left the bag where she found it. The new girlfriend sure looked overweight that first day on the beach. It was like she'd gained ten pounds overnight. There's nothing like too-tight elastic to draw attention to those adorable rolls of fat.

BATHROOM REVENGE

Mindy, a nineteen-year-old psychology undergraduate, struggled with the ethics of targeting revenge on her ex-boyfriend's new sweetie. Her friends told her to go for it. After all, the new sweetie was none other than Mindy's friend who'd stolen the boyfriend away.

Mindy let herself into her ex's home. In the guest bathroom, she took some cling film, wrapped it tightly over the top of the toilet bowl, and then put the seat down. You get the picture – the new babe would use the toilet and end up weeing all over the carpet. She also smeared clear honey (golden syrup works well too) all over the toilet seat.

Here's another toilet-centred revenge story. Yes, it's infantile, but pretty good. A woman placed open packages of ketchup, the kind you get at fast food joints, under the little feet on the underside of the toilet seat so that when the new girlfriend sat down, ketchup would splatter down her legs. Tee hee.

ROSE'S LOVE OIL

Rose knew that her ex had a thing for using baby oil during sex. She'd never really liked feeling like a human french fry but, being a good sport, she had gone along with it anyway.

Rose's revenge cut right to the heart of the matter, and it was definitely below the belt. She surmised that the baby oil would soon be in use with his next bedmate. She found the bottle in the cabinet next to his bed and poured it down the sink. Then she carefully refilled it with a colourless vinaigrette.

FRILLY NOTHINGS

The bedroom is a frequent and obvious target for avengers, especially when the avengee is the kind of attractive rogue who uses his bedroom skills to weave webs around women. One woman suggested that a simple way of sabotaging his new relationship would be to toss a pair of frilly panties under the bed. Sooner or later, the new babe in the sack would find them.

SECRET MESSAGES
This one is good. Karen snuck into her ex-boyfriend's house while he was at work, and using the white phosphorescent paint that glows brightly in the dark, wrote on the ceiling above his bed: 'I love Karen . . . Karen's my perfect lover.' You get the gist.

Since Karen knew her boyfriend was particularly fond of the missionary position and rarely ventured out of his routine, she knew the new girlfriend would be the first to see the words glowing on the ceiling above her like a message straight from God.

LUCILLE'S REVENGE
Lucille was particularly justified in pulling out all the stops in her revenge on the new girlfriend: her replacement was none other than her own sister. All those nights when her boyfriend had stayed up with her sister to watch the late-night film, they'd really been going at it like rabbits as poor unsuspecting Lucille slept in the next room.

When Lucille is pushed, she can become deliciously evil. She got back at them by putting lice eggs on their bed pillows. This made a lasting impression on both of them.

Okay, okay, so we've moved very quickly from slingshots to atomic bombs, but if they have trampled all over your feelings together, then feel free to bring out your killer weapons and blast 'em.

20
Rules About Engagement Rings

Remember all those old rules about giving the engagement ring back if you split up before the marriage? Forget that nonsense! Especially if it's his fault that the relationship went down the toilet. The best revenge in this case: turn the ring in for cash.

Go to the jewellery store. Tell them your fiancé died. Make up some gruesome scenario like he fell into a log-cutting machine and was chopped to pieces, or something similar that involves lots of blood and screaming. Cry if you need to. Through your tears, whimper, 'The ring's all I have left of him. But I need to sell it to cover his funeral expenses.'

Once you get that money in your hot little palm, you'll feel a whole lot better – and so will your bank account. The next step is to turn the cash into something terrific. Choose something you've always wanted but haven't been able to afford, like a trip to Africa or Australia. Bon voyage!

21
He's Marrying Someone Else!

So he's getting married to someone else. He who was so commitment phobic. He who said, 'We don't need marriage. We have something bigger than marriage.' Excuse me while I throw up.

Remember Sally's anguish in *When Sally Met Harry* when she finds out that her longtime live-in boyfriend is marrying the first woman he dated after their break-up? It's this pain that catapults her into sleeping with Harry when their friendly, comforting kisses turn passionate.

Since you probably don't have a Harry on hand, what can you do to get those bad feelings out of your system? Take it from me: confronting him and pleading everlasting love is about as advisable as jumping into the lion pit at the zoo. Confronting her and telling her the truth about what he's really like will also not work; it'll just make you look like a jealous bitch. And you don't want that.

Instead, dwell on the positives, like he's out of your hair forever. Like now he's her problem, not yours. Like she'll soon find out who he really is. Yeah! Right on!

CONNUBIAL BLISS It made Vera sick to hear of the elaborate preparations being made for her ex-boyfriend's sudden wedding to a beautiful young woman from a wealthy American family. What made it especially galling was that this young thing had made it clear that she felt Vera did not even rate as competition, openly flirting with the guy while he and Vera were still together.

The wedding, a major social event with the kind of opulence and trimmings that would make Joan Collins look like a bag lady, was all to take place at a ritzy old hunting lodge in one of America's national parks.

Vera booked herself into the lodge the night before the wedding. She got up before dawn and proceeded to sabotage the hotel's sewage system by plugging up all the toilets with masses of shredded newspaper.

Vera stayed on at the lodge to witness the effect. Sitting in the garden, wearing a large sunhat and dark sunglasses and pretending to read a book, she watched with relish as the hotel management hustled to bring in a truckload of portable toilets, which they hastily set up on the rear lawn.

The wedding cars arrived. The festivities began. And it wasn't long before elegantly dressed but very uneasy wedding guests started to line up in front of the portable toilets. Eventually the bride had to join the line outside the makeshift loos. When it was the bride's turn, Vera watched gleefully as she backed in, struggling to cram her enormous wedding dress into the small space. Then, as if Nature herself had a hand in Vera's revenge, it started to rain and the lawn turned to mud. Vera quietly closed her book and left. A great calmness had descended upon her.

A CHOICE MESSAGE Melissa was faced with a similar predicament. Her boyfriend of seven years was now marrying a woman he'd dated for only four months. The wife-to-be was a Catholic, something Melissa knew would please his overbearing Catholic family no end. His mother was thrilled that he'd dumped the non-Catholic Melissa and was now marrying someone more appropriate. The wedding was to take place in the city cathedral with hundreds of guests in attendance.

Melissa still had a key to his home – she'd had the foresight to have it copied while it was in her possession. The day before the wedding she waited in her car near his block of flats until she saw him leave. Then this bad girl went inside and found the black patent leather shoes he'd be wearing for the ceremony the next day. On one sole she wrote in white paint: 'Big Ego'. On the other: 'Small Dick'.

Since it was a Catholic wedding, Melissa knew at some point during the ceremony he'd have to kneel before the altar. Then her handiwork would provide amusement for the vast audience. Some no doubt would laugh out loud. And he would not have the foggiest idea why.

THE UNINVITED WEDDING GUEST Tara, an

American performance artist, carried on a torrid affair with a supposedly married man for two years. Soon after they broke up, she heard, to her amazement, that he was getting married. He had lied to her all along and had used his phantom marriage as a way to keep her at arm's length. Tara was furious. And who could blame her?

She devised a plan of revenge that was gutsy and bold, and one that perfectly suited her outrageous personality. Tara showed up at the wedding in disguise, posing as a distant cousin. Since it was a large affair, she was able to blend in with the crowd and set about carrying out her revenge.

Tara had brought a lovely silver-wrapped wedding present, which she placed in a prominent position on the gift table. Who was to know that inside the elegantly wrapped package was none other than a dead cat?

She'd also stopped by Hollywood Magic, a famous magic shop on Hollywood Boulevard, and picked up a Groom's Gift Box, which contained 'energy pills', 'a compass to help you find it' and 'a small splint in case you need help', which she left for the groom. (You could go to a joke shop and put together your own 'Groom's Gift Box'.)

Next, she sauntered over to admire the beautiful five-tier wedding cake. When no one was looking, she secretly released a bag of ants onto the icing.

During the sit-down dinner, Tara had fun with another item she'd purchased at the magic shop: an electronic whoopee cushion. She had discreetly hung the speaker device on the back of the groom's chair at the head table. From where she sat she could fire off sounds of flatulence which emanated periodically from the embarrassed married couple. Each assumed the other to be responsible. The new in-laws were less than impressed.

Not one for doing things halfway, Tara waited until it was time for the toasts, and then stood up and congratulated the bride on winning a husband with such well-known sexual prowess.

During the photo session, she managed to blend in to the crowd in most of the wedding photos, discreetly giving the finger to the camera. And after plying the photographer with a stiff drink, she asked him to take a solo picture of her. Just as he clicked his shutter, she swiftly turned and mooned him – another nice little surprise for the couple to discover later.

Finally, she found out from the best man where the couple was going for their honeymoon. Before leaving the reception, she made a few phone calls and managed to cancel both their airline reservations and their hotel accommodations. What a gal!

Gate-crashing a wedding is not for the fainthearted, and it's definitely not recommended if you still harbour delusions of being in love with him. This is only for the girlfriends out there who have a great sense of humour and love to make fun of staid social conventions – the kind who giggled in church as a kid.

WEDDING SABOTAGE Here are a few other things you can do at the blessed event:

Slip into the dining room and place neon condoms under everyone's plate. The stuffy elderly relatives will love them.

If you're feeling extravagant, have your name and his printed on them.

When the bride slips off her suspender, shout, 'Show us your tits!'

In the receiving line, thrust your tongue into his mouth.

In the receiving line, thrust your tongue into her mouth.

Accidentally knock the cake off the table.

If there's an open toast, stand up and shout, 'Geronimo!'

Let a rat loose on the dance floor.

Spill red wine all over the bride's gown.

Ask the women guests to stand up if they've slept with the groom.

Ditto with the male guests and the bride.

Ditto with the male guests and the groom.

Slip a telegram into the pile that will be read aloud at the dinner. Have it be from the bride's old boyfriend saying he's dying of AIDS, or asking her to visit their love child sometime.

Crawl under the dining table and tie his shoelaces together.

While you're under there, unzip his pants.

Make out passionately with the best man.

Pay a child to burst in during the meal and yell out 'Daddy!' as he makes a beeline for the groom.

If you can get your hands on an invite before the wedding, photocopy it and hand it out to the homeless.

Spike the punch with heavy-duty alcohol.

During the reception, creep outside to the wedding car and paint a choice message on the rear window, like: 'Leper colony or bust!' Be sure you're out there in the crowd of guests when the bride and groom get into the car. Smile and clap with everyone else as you secretly savour the look of devastation on his face.

PART THREE
The Rules of Revenge

Now that you've seen what your sisters have accomplished, it's time to turn your attention to devising your own fabulous acts of revenge.

Following are some rules and guidelines to help you in this venture. The goal is to keep you within an ethical framework and on the right side of the law, and to propel you without mishap through the dark jungle of post-relationship fallout and back into the sunshine.

Rule 1:
Be Calm and Rational

A big turning point in life is realizing that you don't have to be tossed around by pain and suffering like flotsam in a stormy sea. When bad things are happening, there is one realm in which you can take charge and gain control, and that is yourself.

Begin by looking in the mirror and saying, 'Calm down, dearie. This will pass. Now what can you do to help yourself through this difficult time?' Then make a deliberate effort to take care of yourself both physically and emotionally.

To help you stay rational, look at what's going on from a cosmic perspective. You're experiencing a kind of death – the death of a relationship. In *On Death and Dying*, Elisabeth Kubler Ross says that if you find out you have a terminal illness and death is looming in your future, you will go through five emotional phases in this sequence: denial, anger, bargaining, depression, and finally acceptance.

In a similar way, when a relationship dies, you pass through an inevitable series of emotions: shock, pain, anger – revenge – catharsis, and healing.

Just as bargaining is vital to the process of coping with death, revenge is the all-important transition that takes us out of the bad stuff and into a new place of self-possession.

Once you've regained your equilibrium channel all your excess emotion into planning and executing a revenge scheme. But don't get ahead of yourself. You'll need to maintain a clear head to pull it off to maximum effect.

Rule 2:
Be Sure the Offence Warrants Revenge

Before plunging headfirst into revenge, ask yourself one simple but fundamental question: is the situation worth all this time and energy? If the answer is no, you're off the hook. Clearly your revenge fantasies have dissipated or have been resolved.

If the answer is yes, look at yourself again in the mirror and firmly ask, 'So what was your role in this debacle? Why did the relationship go off the rails? How much did you contribute to the train wreck?' Be brutally honest with yourself. If the blame can be split equally between both of you, or if you were the bad guy (sorry ladies, occasionally, though rarely, it is the woman's fault), then forget about revenge altogether.

Never ever go against the natural order of things. Remember that revenge is payback. A settling of a score. Getting even. And it is only allowed to enter the picture when the moral universe cries out for retaliation against a wrongdoing. In other words, don't give an enema if there's no gastric upset.

In some circumstances, revenge is inevitable. When lies and betrayal are involved, retaliation is always justified. Even the Old Testament sanctions the returning of evil for evil and blood for blood.

Imagine he just dumped you for your best friend. Or he was two-timing you with a woman who worked in his office building. Or he told you he was away for a week, then you saw him out on the town with one of those annoying women who really look great in a short skirt. In all of these scenarios, revenge is most definitely in order. And the more devastating, the better.

Rule 3:
Be Sure That Your Mark Is Responsible

What if you were to fire off some ugly little missile at your one-time honey only to find out later that he had nothing to do with the wrong-doing, or that it was a legitimate misunderstanding? How embarrassing!

You can guard against such mortifications by always making sure that he's really responsible for the offence. Before going any further, stop and ask yourself the following questions:

1. Did he resort to dirty underhanded tactics?
2. Did he lie, cheat, or steal?
3. Did he treat you with less respect than you deserve?

If the answer to any of the above questions is yes, then go forward without second thoughts.

Rule 4:
Cool Off First

Revenge, as the proverb says, is a dish best served cold. In other words, the avenger should cool off or 'sleep on it' before acting. This is always good advice when we are gripped with raging revenge fantasies. How many of us have rushed into doing something on impulse only to wake up cringing the next morning?

Emotion fuels irrationality. If you act in haste, it's likely to backfire. The best avengers stay cool, calm, and collected. They conserve all their energy for plotting their revenge.

Rule 5:
Make a Plan

Always take time to devise a plan that is worthy of your mark. Then, before going any further, think through every single step. If you need materials, gather them together. Explore all the ways your plan might misfire, or worse, expose you as the perpetrator.

Many revenge plots require access to your ex's home, office, or other personal space, so if possible, don't wait till the relationship is completely over; there's always a period of argument and dissolution before a separation becomes final. When you're emotionally detaching but still have physical access to his domain is the perfect time for hatching your plot.

Once you've made your plan, proceed with ice-cold precision. Rest easy knowing that he will soon get exactly what he deserves.

Rule 6:
Use Your Creativity

Use this opportunity to let all your untapped creativity shine through. The goal is to come up with a unique act of revenge that's perfectly tailored to your guy, one that will really push his personal buttons, one he'll never forget.

Hit him hard in his most vulnerable area – whether it be a cherished possession or a personal weakness he confided to you in an intimate moment. Most of all, you want to come up with something that will be emotionally satisfying for you.

Try not to resort to hackneyed old revenge acts like slashing tires. Yawn. Tactics like this are not only boring, they won't have the desired impact on your mark. Revenge can and should be deliciously imaginative. Remember the horse head in the bed in *The Godfather*, an unforgettable *tour de force* that hit the reader of the novel (and the viewer of the film) right between the eyes. For many of us those blood-soaked bed sheets remain an indelible memory. Now no one is suggesting you resort to animal brutality in planning your revenge. Just let your creativity blossom.

Rule 7:
Keep It in the Fun Zone

Revenge fantasies can be excessive and extreme and cause lots of pain and suffering for your mark. But the real thing should always be lighthearted and fun. For example, you can daydream all you like about releasing a boa constrictor that hasn't eaten for a month inside his home. But should you ever really do such a thing?

Just keep in mind that revenge is a hurdle to be crossed on the road to mental health and personal empowerment, and if you can laugh about your ex, you're already well along the road to recovery. Coping with life's problems with humour is always the best way to go. Laughter is the greatest healer of all.

Never ever become psychotic. Know the distinction between therapeutic revenge and destructive revenge. One is healthy, the other is not. If you find yourself obsessing with thoughts of revenge, seek therapy.

Remember Jean Harris, the woman who didn't seek therapy and ended up killing her lover, Herman Tarnower, the Scarsdale doctor? It's a fascinating story recounted in Diana Trilling's book *Mrs. Harris*, which should be compulsory reading for all adolescent girls. A cultured and stylish headmistress, Mrs. Harris struggled to cope with her womanizing lover. The daughter of a cold authoritarian father, she was in the grip of the wounds of her childhood. Instead of simply telling the pig to take a hike, Mrs. Harris slid deeper and deeper into the depths of self-abasement and finally violence. Like Captain Ahab in *Moby Dick*, she became so consumed with the monster that she herself became the monster.

By the time she entered the doctor's bedroom, a gun in one hand and a bunch of flowers in the other, she had truly descended into the state described by Yeats as 'the foul rag-and-bone shop of the heart'.

If you ever find yourself even glimpsing into dark shadowy areas like this, go to your doctor immediately and demand a supply of those serotonin boosters that, in my opinion, should be dispensed in public toilets alongside the Tampax and condoms.

Rule 8:
Choose Your Weapons

Double-check that you are drawing on the correct weapon level in your revenge arsenal. Never waste a first-rate revenge act on a small potatoes crime. And don't get carried away with delusions of megalomania. Sorry, life isn't a video game. You can't hit a button and obliterate an entire landscape and every living thing on it every time someone makes you feel bad.

Also, take care never to put yourself in your own line of fire. Remember that cinematic ode to marriage, *The War of the Roses*. Kathleen Turner and Michael Douglas fire off some superb revenge acts – he saws the heels off all her shoes, she smashes his car with a truck, he urinates in the fish she's about to serve to her dinner guests, she pretends to make pâté out of his pet dog. In the end, they barricade themselves in their house and end up plunging to their deaths from a huge chandelier. So who's the winner? No one.

If you're dealing with a small-time offender, get revenge on him which befits his insignificant position. Don't let this pipsqueak think he ever had the ability to really get to you. Save your major league weapons for those big-time heart-breakers and transgressions.

Rule 9:
Don't Break the Law

One rule can't be overemphasized: *never* resort to illegal acts in your revenge. Getting arrested, or worse, going to jail, is not worth it. You'll be the loser. Don't forget the ice-skater Tonya Harding. No matter what she does to try to redeem herself – even giving mouth-to-mouth resuscitation to a choking old lady in a restaurant (some claim it was staged) – she will never ever shake off that life-defining moment when she allegedly plotted the clubbing of Nancy Kerrigan's leg.

Remember that wonderful scene in Terry McMillan's novel and film, *Waiting to Exhale*. After Bernardine's husband has announced that he's leaving her, she tosses all of his clothes into his BMW and sets the car on fire. She then has a $1 garage sale to get rid of all his other possessions and yells to her absent husband, 'Since you want to start a new life, motherf—, see what starting from scratch feels like.'

The burning BMW scene was a high point of the story. It elicited screams of laughter and empathy from women readers and viewers. It was vivid. It was primal. And it hit the male character right where it hurt – his beloved material possessions literally went up in smoke.

But don't forget that life is life and films are films. Don't rush out and duplicate Bernardine's glorious expurgation. The truth is, burning a car can get you in big trouble, especially if it explodes and sets the entire neighbourhood on fire. The same goes for that unforgettable movie moment when Thelma and Louise avenge the lascivious lorry driver by blowing up his lorry. Try blowing up a lorry and see what happens.

In real life, always know the difference between being an avenger and being a terrorist. Temper your acts so you never do any lasting damage to a person or property. For example, if you have to graffiti his car, be sure you do it with washable spray paint. Don't deface something permanently, or his revenge might be much sweeter than yours.

There are, of course, some situations where you can use the legal system to help you. After all, the courts are the arena for some of our most socially sanctioned acts of revenge. In some countries, isn't the death penalty the ultimate revenge?

In sum, try to choose a playful, legally sound remedy that: a. gets the point across; b. gives you a feeling of satisfaction; and c. helps you reach your ultimate goal – catharsis.

Rule 10:
Beware of Innocent Bystanders

We've already talked about not blatantly harming an innocent new girlfriend, or if he's married, his spouse. Avengers should also be wary of fallout that might injure other types of innocent third parties: his colleagues, family members, and friends. For example, don't wreak revenge on his home if it will also affect an innocent roommate. Don't lob a stink bomb into his office if there are other people there. Always keep your sights trained on the real villain.

Rule 11:
Cover Your Tracks

Covering your tracks means paying attention to anything that could be used against you should he decide to be a weasel and blow the whistle on you. You don't want to end up in the middle of a lawsuit. While he may suspect you are behind the assault, take a tip from the Sphinx. Remain silent and inscrutable. Also follow these guidelines:

Don't use your own phone.

Don't use your own computer account.

Don't use credit cards or personal cheques to purchase supplies.

Don't blab to everybody about what you're doing: 'Loose lips sink ships.'

Don't break the law.

Don't wear perfume if you're entering his home or office.

Don't let anyone witness what you're doing.

Don't involve a third person – like a doorman or his secretary – who might snitch on you.

Don't call his answering machine afterwards and laugh like a maniac. This is very important. If you run into him, resist the temptation to thumb your nose or to jump up and down with glee.

Rule 12:
Execute Your Plan Carefully

Last but not least, don't go ahead with your plan unless you're fully committed to what you're doing. If you have any qualms about the morality of revenge, work them out first. Be completely honest about the whole dirty business. Even though we teach our children to 'turn the other cheek' and 'never hit back', do we ever really mean it? Hell, no!

Now that your conscience is clear and you're as focused as a jackal, you're ready to put your fully formulated plan in motion. Follow it to a tee. Don't get carried away in the heat of the moment. Don't improvise or go over the top. Remember, you've thought it all through already. Now it's time for the execution, so to speak. Enjoy every splendid black moment.

PART FOUR
Catharsis

22
Healthier Alternatives

Believe it or not, there are healthier solutions to resolving revenge impulses than acting on them.

Like in real estate, the overall goal here is closure, closure, closure. An end to uneasy emotions, a settling of the score. Don't get stuck. Get on with your life. Workplace homicides like those that erupt in American post offices are all products of people getting trapped in a bad state of mind.

Never forget Glenn Close's character in *Fatal Attraction*, the epitome of what *not* to be when in the grip of revenge. Talk about letting yourself go. And bear in mind that very occasionally, revenge can be transformed into forgiveness.

HOW TO CULTIVATE INNER PEACE One
alternative way of getting bad feelings off your chest is action-oriented personal therapy. This provides several benefits: you don't have to have any contact with him; no one witnesses your ravings; and best of all, you can have a lot of fun.

For example, you could kick a Barney doll till the stuffing comes out while you sing the Barney theme song: 'I hate you. . . . You hate me. . . . We're a dys-func-tion-al fam-i-ly. . . .' Or you could drop a watermelon off the roof of a tall building and imagine it's your mark's head exploding on the concrete below.

PHOTOGRAPHS OF HIM Isn't it horrible when you have all those photographs of someone who's essentially turned into a big tumour in your life? Forget looking through them nostalgically and sighing about the good old days. This is a big no-no that's guaranteed to lead you down the road of sentimentality and regret. *You do not want to go there*.

Here's what to do with the photographs. Set aside a cosy evening at home. Gather all the photographs together. Destroy all the pictures of him, except for the ones where he looks ugly or geeky. Hang on to these – you can use them down the road to congratulate yourself on having gotten away from such a potentially bad gene pool.

Now it's time to slowly burn the photographs. You'll enjoy watching the flames licking across his body and melting his face into goo.

If there are some nice group shots that you want to keep, just cut him out with scissors. For extra fun, substitute his head with paste-ins of Yanni, O.J., Noel Edmonds – any of your least favourite people.

Other ways to trash the pictures: tape his photograph to a train track and watch a train roll over it. You could tape his photo to a bowling ball and take him bowling, or you could toss his photo off a motorway overpass and watch his mug be run over . . . and over . . . and over.

TURN THE OTHER CHEEK Ultimately, the best revenge is to turn the other cheek, to do nothing, to accept

the fact that he's a worm and move on. This is the sweetest revenge of all because it shows you are above and beyond having an emotional reaction to your enemy. He is no longer able to affect you. Hooray! You have achieved the goal of all revengers – catharsis. And if you forgive your enemies it just might drive them crazy. Be warned, however: this is hard to fake.

23
Care Packages for the Recently Dumped

The period following the death of a relationship is critical in terms of recovery. It's a roller-coaster time packed with conflicting emotions like regret, indecision, exuberance, happiness, and sadness. It's vitally important to take care of oneself during this time and hasten the return to a healthy equilibrium.

What follows is a plan detailing a sequence of care packages designed for the postbreak-up period. Think of them as applying balm to your wounds.

Doing this for yourself is great therapy, but if you find yourself emotionally paralyzed or sitting in a dark room muttering, enlist a girlfriend to deliver your recovery supplies. Promise you'll do the same for her next time she's in a love funk.

Treat the postbreak-up period like a time of withdrawal after going off drugs, when you'll have to resist the urge to reach for another fix – in other words, to grab the phone and beg him to come over. Know that this is a time when you will suffer and be irrational. But bear with it, because once you pass through the flames and out the other side, you'll feel a million times better.

WEEK ONE

This is the most painful time. Your brain is scrambled. Emotions are bruised and raw. The wounds are gushing blood. Week one's care package should therefore contain the following items:

1. This book. Vital for anyone with a trampled heart.
2. Your baby blanket or teddy bear. Bury your face in it and howl. Just be sure the windows are closed tight and no one's around to witness this. You don't want to get taken away to the loony bin.
3. Schmaltzy tearjerker films. These will get the tears flowing and draw all that excess emotion out, like pus out of a wound.
4. A jumbo box of soft perfumed tissues to wipe away the tears, even if they are tears of joy that he's finally out of your life.
5. Slow-burning logs for the fireplace. This is the time to huddle around the fire and stare tragically into the flames. If you don't have a fireplace, you can buy mail-order from America the Videotape Fire-Place. This surreal video is just a two-hour static shot of a burning fire, complete with realistic crackling sounds. (See Appendix for mail-order information.)
6. Ice cream. Lots of it. The richer the better. My personal recommendation is Ben and Jerry's Cherry Garcia. Yum.
7. A big box of Godiva chocolates. If you can't indulge now, when can you? This is the time to pig out big time.
8. A supply of pink lightbulbs. It's important to avoid harsh lights when a glance at your haggard reflection in the mirror could send you running for the sleeping pills. Soft rosy lighting will make you look

your best and give your melancholia a romantic moodiness.

9. Opera recordings. You can lip sync the tragic parts like Madame Butterfly's death scene – it'll help to put your puny little problems in their proper context.

10. Hypnosis tapes for use while asleep. Have them programmed with ego-boosting propaganda like 'he's not worthy of you', 'he's a dick', and other subtle reminders of your new world picture.

11. A week's supply of delivered dinners. You'll feel too horrible to cook.

12. A crate of fruit-flavoured carbonated water – to go with the meal. Keep away from alcohol in these early vulnerable days. Alcohol brings on excessive emotion and encourages impulsive actions.

13. Tape for you to seal your mouth shut whenever you feel the urge to grab the phone and call him.

14. Instructions for turning off the phone. That way you won't have to waste time and energy anguishing if he does call – or agonizing if he doesn't. You'll simply never know. And ignorance is bliss.

WEEK TWO
Week two can be just as tough as week one – for some, it can be even tougher. There have been no phone calls begging for reconciliation. No bouquets left on your doorstep. No threats of suicide if you won't return. Looks like he's gone for good. By week two it's very important to get ahold of yourself and put all your emotional energy into exorcising any traces of him. The care package for week two should therefore contain:

1. Matches. With these, burn anything that belongs to him or that reminds you of him. Be careful, however,

not to burn the house down.

2. Paper shredder. Shred all his sickening lie-filled letters.

3. Plasticine. Make little models of him. You can stick them with pins, gouge out their eyes, or rip their heads off.

4. Videos with strong independent female leads played by actresses like Bette Davis or Katherine Hepburn. These are excellent role models – tremendously successful, very singular women who have done just fine, thank you, without permanent male attachments.

5. Long Russian novels like *War and Peace* or *Anna Karenina*. This will help you transport your mind to a faraway place and time during those long evening hours you now spend alone.

WEEK THREE It's now time to concentrate on action, things you can do to deliberately move forward in your new life. To aid you with this new impetus, the care package for week three should include the following:

1. Phone numbers of the killer divorce attorneys in town. You're calm enough now to have a rational discussion about where to go from here and whether or not you can take his home, his car, and everything he owns with you.

2. A big stack of travel brochures. Now's the time to take a well-deserved holiday doing something exotic or unusual, like riding camels in Morocco or canoeing on the Amazon. Be sure you enlist an outgoing friend to go with you so you don't feel lonesome.

3. A day at a serious health spa where they offer rigorous salt rubs. There's nothing like a good exfoliation

(dead-skin removal) to make one feel renewed. Reptiles naturally go through this process quite often. We humans need more help. While you're at the spa, why not splurge on the whole package? Get the manicure, pedicure, facial – the works.

4. A diet plan to shed the pounds you gained pigging out on all that chocolate and ice cream during week one.

5. A makeover, including a fabulous new haircut.

6. A puppy or a kitten, something on which to lavish all that unfocused love and affection. This is not recommended for everyone. While pets are often very cute, they do introduce a new responsibility in your life that you may not want to take on right now. If you want to take off impulsively for a weekend to enjoy your new freedom, you have to make sure that someone will be around to walk and feed Rover.

7. A disguise kit including a wig, nose, and glasses, just in case you run into the unmentionable one on the street.

8. Pepper spray in case he recognizes you.

9. A book of curses. Focus that late night energy in a constructive direction.

10. A voodoo doll – an excellent outlet for venom and aggression.

WEEK FOUR You're ready to live your life fully again.
Week four is the time to launch headlong into your terrific new future. This care package will help propel you forward. In here, pack:

1. A blind date. But be careful with this. Do not mention your recent break-up. Do not drink too much and start weeping. If you're in a restaurant, do not

pound your fist on the table or fling your plate across the room. Definitely do not jump in the sack with him. Compensatory sex is never a good idea.

2. A catalogue of university courses. Now's a great time to embark on self-improvement, whether you want to learn something fun like how to fly fish or start that MBA programme to move on to your second career.

3. Music lessons. You always wanted to learn how to play the violin or the piano but never had the time. Now's the perfect opportunity. You may also find playing an instrument soothing to your rattled emotions.

4. Tango lessons. This is fun, great exercise, and a good way to meet new people. Okay, so it's unlikely you'll run into some dashing stud down at the local night club, but a quick twirl around the floor with a funny balding shoe salesman may be just what the doctor ordered.

5. Enrolment in a nature club. Ask about local Sunday morning hikes which are a big favourite with urban singles.

6. A gift voucher for new lingerie. Sexy new undies always boost a woman's spirits.

7. A personalized number plate. This is a good way for ex-wives and ex-girlfriends to flaunt their freedom. A nicely worded plate not only makes a statement, it provides amusement for fellow sisters out on the road. Here are a few favourites:

DUMPMEN
FEMRULE
BYEDICK
EXAPUTZ
SINGLE
MANGONE
FREEDOM

24
Celebrate!

Celebrate your liberation by throwing a divorce or break-up party. It will give you an opportunity to indulge in some wonderful and therapeutic games, and will also get you back in touch with the pleasure of being with your female friends.

REVENGE PARTY GAMES

Run the wedding video backwards to symbolically undo the union.

Cut him out of all the wedding photos – or use them to play pin the tail on the groom.

Stomp on that piece of wedding cake you kept in the freezer.

Trash photographs of him: stick pins in his eyeballs, slice off his ears, rip off his lips, stick dead flies in his mouth.

Go around the room encouraging party guests to reveal the one thing they couldn't stand about him. Tell them not to hold back.

Burn your wedding veil.

Buy an old mannequin, dress it in your ex's clothes, and allow your guests to let loose all their primitive instincts in defacing and humiliating him. Tape his photo onto the face. Let them throw jam, the contents of the cat litter box, anything they want at the dummy. Depending on the wildness of your friends, or the number of martinis all of you drink, you could provide knives, axes, or acetylene blowtorches, for a total blowout carnage celebration.

When you're done with all this childish but wonderfully satisfying acting out, accept what has happened and move on. Remember the old adage, 'Living well is the best revenge.'

25
Moving On

Congratulations! You're free! And one nice consequence of revenge is that there's no turning back. Once the revenge act is complete, never ever linger to:

Repeat the act.

Gloat in front of your target.

Think of even uglier acts of revenge. There's a fine line between revenge and harassment. You don't want to turn into a psycho.

Hope that your target will fall to his knees and beg forgiveness. He won't. The relationship was over with whatever he did to piss you off.

Your act of revenge is the last nail in the coffin. Go ahead and bury the relationship. If need be, take a photo of him and literally dig a hole and cover him with dirt – and don't come back every weekend to put fresh flowers on the grave.

Last, but not least, protect yourself. Never ever put yourself in a vulnerable position with your mark again. He is toast as far as you're concerned.

You can now move on to new battlegrounds and new adversaries. Right on, girlfriend! You did it! You took control of your life!

PART FIVE
Starting Over

While in the throes of a failed relationship, it's impossible to imagine venturing into a new one. But guess what? Sooner or later, most of us come snuffling back to the well of love.

Be very careful, however. Don't leap too quickly into a new relationship or you'll run the risk of dragging all that moth-eaten baggage into your new situation.

Consider, instead, enjoying the time you have alone. Use this free time for refuelling, nurturing yourself, and getting your feet planted firmly on the ground again.

26
The Dos and the Don'ts

One of the advantages of having a horrible love experience is that one is a better person for it, right? At least that's the theory. After getting rid of all that lingering venom via an act of revenge, you should now be in better control of your emotions. You're more mature. The pack of wild dogs that was your psyche should, by now, be on a short leash, gripped tightly in your hot little fist.

In case you need a few guidelines as you toil onward in the trenches of love, here are a few dos and don'ts to bear in mind.

DON'T REMINISCE
Indulging in reminiscence is a real no-no. Never ever yearn for the good times you had together. Write down everything he did to screw up the relationship. Carry it with you at all times. Read it while waiting at traffic lights, at lunch time, whenever you lapse into selective memory. Another good idea is to employ a strategy used by Alcoholics Anonymous. Ask a girlfriend if you can call her whenever you have a desperate urge to see him.

DO DWELL ON HIS SHORTCOMINGS Concentrate on all his annoying little habits and quirks that used to drive you crazy. For example:

Muttering 'ca-ching!' like a cash register when you order an expensive item on the menu.

Squeezing his zits in front of you.

Picking his nose in the car.

Scratching his family jewels in public.

Watching Rambo videos over and over.

Forgetting your birthday.

Watching the Home Shopping Channel for hours on end.

Thinking a brioche is a piece of jewellery.

Farting in his sleep.

Snoring.

Drooling on the pillow.

Drooling on you.

Belching.

Singing Barry Manilow songs in the shower.

Smelling his socks when he takes them off.

Yelling at the TV.

Sucking up spaghetti one strand at a time.

Eating gristle.

Crunching through chicken bones.

Kissing his dog on the lips.

Calling his cat lovecakes.

Never helping carry your shopping bags from the car.

Looking in the mirror every chance he gets.

Spending hours on the computer.

Picking his teeth with his fingernail.

Trimming his toenails while watching TV.

Licking his dessert plate when he thinks you're not looking.

Singing along with the Beach Boys in a falsetto voice.

Mooning other drivers on the motorway.

Putting his feet up on the dinner table.
Eating food left over on the next table in a restaurant.
Snapping his fingers to get a waiter's attention.
Treating shop assistants like they're the scum of the earth.
Muttering obscenities under his breath whenever he sees a
    nun.
Worshipping his mother.

WHAT IF I RUN INTO MY EX IN A RESTAURANT AND HE'S WITH A DATE?

Don't
Burst into tears.
Tell an off-colour joke.
Lose bladder control.
Ask how his mother is.
Start discussing the kids' report cards.
Talk about how much the dog misses him.
Beg him to come back to you.
Weep uncontrollably.
Tell him you miss him.
Stammer.
Hyperventilate.
Thump your chest shouting, 'ooga-booga'.
Faint.
Start barking uncontrollably.
Run from the room crying.
Bleed from the hands and feet.
Faint and fall headfirst into the mashed potatoes.
Sweat.
Start talking in tongues.
Fall to your knees and genuflect.
Break out in hives.

Projectile vomit.

Develop a facial tic.

Thrust his date's head into a chocolate cake.

Accidentally smash a cream pie in her face.

Pretend you have amnesia.

Ask if you left your retainer under the pillow.

Break into a tap dancing routine.

Rub yourself up against the waiter and moan in ecstasy.

Have a spontaneous orgasm.

Spit on them both.

Get down on your hands and knees and try to crawl away.

Run crying into the ladies' toilets.

Ask him how the cat is.

Hug them both and say you hope you can all be friends.

Tell him how much you miss his mother.

Ask her for coffee so you can discuss his shortcomings.

Ask how the penile implants are holding up.

Ask if he got the tests back yet (with a look of concern and a knowing little wink).

Tell him your sister had a baby, then start to cry.

Blurt out that you're pregnant.

Sit on his lap.

Sit on her lap.

Ask her who her plastic surgeon is.

Run outside and key his car.

Drag her to the ladies' toilets and punch her lights out.

Do

Smile warmly and shake both their hands.

Concentrate on his bad features, like those bristly hairs sticking out of his ears.

Whisper loudly in his ear, 'She's not plain, she's adorable.'

Slip him a packet of breath mints.

Tell him he has spinach stuck between his teeth.

Tell him he has something hanging out of his nose.

Slip his date a tube of hair removing cream.
Brush the dandruff off his shoulders.
Accidentally knock a glass of ice water into his crotch.
Remark how much his date resembles his mother.
Ask if that's the tie you gave him for his birthday.
Slip her a tampon with a knowing sisterly wink, pointing to the stain on the seat cushion.
Ask if you left your diaphragm in his bathroom cabinet.
Stare at her chest and ask if they're silicon.

27
His New Role

His new role in your life opens up some subtle revenge opportunities with several nice side benefits. Maintaining a relationship is not recommended for avengers who are still catapulted into throes of emotion whenever they're in the presence of their once beloved. For those of you who are emotionally clear and ready for some entertainment at your ex's expense, read on.

You can call him and ask for his help in doing a variety of activities for which you need his manly skills. You know, the fun stuff like carrying your new sofa up two flights of stairs, helping to move your fridge to a new position in the kitchen – anything that's physically challenging.

As you watch him puffing and sweating, reduced to a brute of brawn and muscle, you can chuckle gleefully. Milk the role of being the weaker sex as you inwardly revel in having put him in his proper place in life: low on the totem pole of evolution. And if the poor dear throws his back out, gloat inwardly, knowing it'll put a significant crimp in his love life. Never laugh derisively out loud or he'll be out of there in a flash.

Here are a few favours you may sweetly request:

Install a mirror. Once he arrives, explain in a matter-of-fact way that you want it on the ceiling over your bed.

Ask him to help you put together a fabulous new king-size bed. When he moves the old bed, have him find a condom wrapper for a brand he doesn't use. Act flustered as you pick it up, blushing.

Replace your old toilet with a new one. Imply he'll be assisting the plumber, who'll mysteriously not show up.

Call him up and ask nicely, 'Would you mind looking after my cat and watering my plants while I fly to Venice with my new boyfriend?'

Have him help you carry boxes of unwanted rubbish out to the bins. Include letters from him visibly poking out through the top.

Ask him to scrape the dead squirrel off your driveway. Afterwards give him a rag to wipe off his dirty hands. Have it be a pair of his Calvin Klein underwear left at your home. When he comments on this, ask innocently, 'Are these yours? I wasn't sure who they belonged to.'

While he's working, have a big bouquet of flowers delivered to yourself. Glance at the card with a little smile of pleasure.

Have one of your girlfriends call, pretending to be a new suitor. Have an intimate chat, discussing your plans for your first weekend away together.

Be sure you look terrific. If you've lost five pounds, show it off. Wear that skimpy Donna Karan T-shirt or those black leather high boots from Gucci.

Be packing an overnight bag as you talk. Offer no explanation as to where you are going.

If you must rub it in, slip your diaphragm into your purse when you see out of the corner of your eye that he's watching you.

Leave a man's razor in the bathroom. Offer him a big glass of water so he'll have to go in there to empty his bladder.

In a lighthearted way, ask him if he'd mind introducing you to that cute new guy in his office.

If you want to be really cold, don't even be there when he shows up. Leave him a note telling him exactly what to do.

Warning: Never use any of these devices as a ploy to get him back. That is pathetic and degrading. No man changes overnight. And you don't want to repeat the same old sad drama.

28
Questions Commonly Asked by Newly Single Women

If you've been in a relationship for a while, the sudden liberation into the world of the unattached can be scary and exhilarating all at once. The following are questions often raised by newly single women.

SHOULD I DISPOSE OF HIS BELONGINGS?

Absolutely and unequivocally – YES. After one woman's significant other departed, she gave his favourite cashmere jumper to her cat to use as a new bed. If you can think up some good uses for his stuff – say like using his favourite CDs as coasters – terrific. Otherwise, treat it as junk and get rid of it.

If you want to make a little cash, go to a car boot sale and sell it all. Or toss it into a raging fire. Think of this as though you're burning everything after a plague has struck. This can be therapeutic in a very primitive way – and enjoy all that extra wardrobe and drawer space that is now all yours.

Things to Keep
House
Car
Friends
Football season tickets
Wine cellar
Bank account
Power drill
Lawn mower
Credit cards
All electronic equipment
Rolling Stones tickets
Computer
Ice cream maker
Cleaning lady
Jewellery
Art
Savings account
Silver and crystal
Braun food processor
Time-share holiday home
Espresso machine
Camping gear
Jumper cables
The Spode china he inherited from his mother
Lottery tickets
Barbecue grill
Pizza stone
Rare book collection
Massage chair
Personal masseuse
His Avirex leather bomber jacket

Things to Trash
Love letters
Photos
Cutesy little stuffed animals
Boring birthday gifts
Sex aids
Dried flowers from your first date
Wedding mementos
List of names you made up together for the children you'll
     thankfully never have
Your honeymoon scrapbook
The phone numbers of all his boring friends you never have
     to see again
His favourite armchair
His wagon wheel coffee table
His polyester 'silk' sheets
His country music collection
His box of photos of old girlfriends
His beer can collection
His secret stash of hair-loss treatment cream
His video game collection
His velvet Elvis painting
His collection of *Reader's Digest* condensed bestsellers

HOW LONG 'TIL I FEEL LIKE MY OLD SELF?

Of course it depends on your personality. Some of us fall off the horse and just get right back on again. Others seem wired for angst and depression. Generally speaking, you can probably expect one month of fallout and suffering for every year you were together.

Don't be in too much of a hurry. Give yourself time to 'find yourself', to 'get in touch with your anger', to stop talking in annoying clichés. Then when you're primed and ready to hunt down the next *objet d'amour*, take the time to separate the wheat from the chaff. That will increase your odds of not falling into yet another fiasco that ends with you back where you started, plotting revenge on some jerk.

WHEN SHOULD I START DATING? If there's nothing good on television, and you've cried all you can cry, the day after the break-up.

WHAT KIND OF MAN SHOULD I LOOK FOR NEXT? How do you describe a good man? Maybe it's best to talk about negative signs that are obvious alarms. If he exhibits any of the following characteristics, you should disappear faster than a polar bear in a snowstorm.

AVOID ANY MAN WHO . . .

Calls you stupid nicknames like Pooky or Snookums on your first date.

Reaches in his pocket for his wallet and a bunch of condoms falls out on the floor.

Takes you for dinner at the McDonald's drive-thru and orders two Happy Meals.

Uses these opening lines: 'I think the alphabet should be rearranged so that u and I are together'; 'Do you believe in love at first sight or do I have to walk by you again?'; 'My wife is dying of cancer'; 'I'm not sure I can love again'; 'I'm finally in touch with my inner child'; 'You remind me of my nursery school teacher'; 'You look like you were born to bear babies.'

Lives with his mother.

On your first date, talks obsessively about his ex-wife while frantically rolling bread pellets between his fingers.

Carries a moth-eaten teddy bear everywhere with him.

Shows up for your first date wearing a T-shirt that says 'Will Work for Sex'.

Has a number plate frame that reads: 'So Many Women, So Little Time.'

Has a beaded evening gown hanging in his wardrobe.

Shaves his armpits.

Wears a thong.

Says he's between careers.

Can't pass a credit check.

Throws up if you mention the word commitment.

Has holes in his underpants.

Watches porno.

Tells you not to order the 'soup du jour' – he tried it once and it was awful.

Can't cook.

Can't change a tyre.

Is a member of the Richard Simmons fan club.

Is president of the Richard Simmons fan club.

Attends Promise Keepers rallies.

On your first date, takes the straw out of his milkshake and showers you with spit balls.

Shops at Woolworths.

Says he's seeking release of his wild man.

Wears women's underwear.

Compulsively reads billboards out loud while driving.

Wears a frilly apron when he cooks.

Drives a Yugo or a Kia.

Loves to shop at Ikea.

Has a Chia pet. (Notice the common thread – avoid him if ANY of his favourite products or stores end in 'ee-yah.')

Knows the names of soap opera characters.

Doesn't like the Rolling Stones.

Kicks puppies.

Kicks babies.
Tells his dog 'Mummy's here!' when you go to his home.
Only has to shave once a week.
Wears a toupee but swears he doesn't.
Makes loud sucking noises when eating.
Makes loud braying noises during sex.
Mutters his ex-wife's name in his sleep.
Mutters his best friend's name in his sleep.
Will never ever sleep over in your bed.
Talks about ex-sex partners all the time.
Thinks Janet Reno is one hot babe.
Makes his cleaning lady call him 'sir'.
Makes fun of his secretary's fat thighs.
Uses eyeliner.
Hates deodorant.
Frequently leaves his wallet at home.
Has one huge unbroken eyebrow.
Has food splatters on his glasses.
Licks his glasses to clean them.
Sucks food stains off his tie.
Hides in women's bathrooms.
Sniffs bicycle seats.
Gets so excited watching *Grandstand* that he ejaculates.
Says he wants to marry Kathie Lee.
Has a thighmaster
Thinks June Whitfield is a bitch.
Hates children.
Secretly tries to date your girlfriends.
Sucks lollipops.
Drools.
Twitches.
Has halitosis.
Has a pet poodle called Shirley.
Has a wobbly butt.
Has hips wider than his shoulders.

Loves mindless puns like 'hair today, gone tomorrow'.
Is called Jon, Chaz, or Vyktor.
Sings along with adverts.
Eats Frosties for breakfast.
Keeps a tally of all the women he's ever slept with.
Is thirty-six and still a virgin.
Loves show tunes.
Gives his entire life history on the first date.
Thinks he's led a fascinating life.
Calls himself an underachiever.
Says whenever it's Christmas and he hears Santa Claus say, 'Ho, ho, ho,' he thinks of his ex-wife (think about it).
Says his ex was his one true love.
On the first date, begs to spend the night, 'just to sleep'.
Lays his head on your breast and weeps.
Attempts to suckle at every opportunity.
Reveals he has a horde of guns and rifles stashed at home.
Has a ring in his penis.
Reveals that he's had a sex change.
Says he was institutionalized for violence as a child.
Has had a lobotomy.
Is heavily medicated.
Always orders the cheapest thing on the menu.
Orders lobster, then asks the waiter if he can lift it out of the tank and bash its brains out.
Eats the green stuff inside lobsters.
Cracks crabs legs with his teeth.
Orders steak tartare then licks up the blood.
Has no reflection in the mirror.
Always has a lovebite.
Wears earmuffs.
Knits.
Explains why he can't get an erection: 'It's not you, it's my medication.'
Throws up after every meal.

Has a portrait of Hitler hanging over his fireplace.

Is pen pals with Charles Manson.

Weeps when he sees the pope.

Has chronic diarrhoea.

Carries a purse.

Calls the bathroom 'the little boys' room'.

Says 'Feelings' is his favourite song.

Will only eat food that is white.

Breeds boa constrictors.

After dinner, flosses his teeth at the table.

When talking to women, stares at their breasts.

Squirts breath freshener in his mouth, then tries to kiss you.

Whips out a calculator at the end of the evening, tallies up the night's expenses, and asks you to pay half.

When discussing his ex-wife, says, 'Some women need to be slapped.'

Asks you in all seriousness who is your favourite Spice Girl.

Calls his penis Norman.

Calls his penis Mr. Happy.

GOOD LUCK OUT THERE

Good luck out there, girlfriends. It's a jungle for sure. I hope this book has helped you hack your way through the gnarly tangles of your own personal crisis, and that you've discovered new, wonderful things about yourself in the process. At the very least, isn't it comforting to know that you are definitely not alone? Just remember . . . laughing at a guy is the best revenge of all.

A Consumer's Guide to Revenge: Products and Services

MAIL-ORDER COMPANIES
Most cities have joke shops, hardware or hobby shops where you can purchase revenge products. Check the Yellow Pages for the ones in your area. An easy and discreet alternative is to purchase via mail order. Following is a sampling of mail-order companies in the UK and USA.

Chemicals and pyrotechnic paraphernalia
Iowa Pyro Supply
1000 130th Street
Stanwood, IA 52337
USA
Tel: 00 1 (319) 945 6637

Rats
Choose from small, regular or large. Packed in units of 20, 25 or 40.

Honeybrook Farm Animal Foods
Honey Brook Farm
Shinehill Lane

South Littleton
Evesham
Worcestershire
WR11 5TP
Tel: (01386) 830 089
Fax: (01386) 833 609
www.users.globalnet.co.uk/~hbrook

Stink bombs, laxative sugar, slime, cigarette bangers, Revenge-O-Gram (plastic doggie 'souvenir' delivered in a box with a personal message) and other jokes.
Jester Limited
P.O. Box 190
Grimston
Kings Lynn
PE32 1GB

Electronic whoopee cushions, Groom's Gift Box and other tricks
Hollywood Magic
6614 Hollywood Blvd.
Hollywood, CA 90028
USA
Tel: 00 1 (213) 464 5610

Spy gadgets, locksmith equipment, James Bond goodies
London Counter Spy Shop
62 Audley Street
London
W1Y 5FB
Tel: (0207) 408 0287
Fax: (0207) 629 9538
www.londonspyshop.com

Micro
5A Parson Street
Hendon
London
NW4 1QA
Tel: (0208) 202 4777
Fax: (0208) 202 4337
www.microelec.com

Sexually explicit photo processing
IMP Photo Services
P.O. Box 141052
Staten Island
NY 10314-1052
USA
Tel: 00 1 (718) 447 1771
www.galexo.com/imp

Videotape fireplace
With holiday music: Digital Video Entertainment, Inc.
Port Saint Lucie
FL 34985
USA

Without holiday music: The Maine InterNet and
Book Shop
561 Lindsey Road
Wells, ME 04090
USA
bennet@cybertours.com

THE INTERNET
There are a number of web sites that are designed to provide
advice and materials for acts of revenge.

alt.revenge

This news group discusses means and methods of revenge. Participants talk about schemes, exchange ideas, and help each other solve problems. People might post articles describing a specific problem. Their goal is 'to make revenge look a bit more like an art form'.

The Avengers Handbook

The best schemes posted in alt.revenge are collected in a big text file called 'The Avengers Handbook'. It can be retrieved from the Avengers Front Page at www.ekran.no/html/revenge

The Ex's Club

Membership to this amazing club, Ex-Lovers.com, allows you to: post nude photos of and stories about your ex; get tips on how to know if your spouse is cheating; track down surveillance equipment; get information about child support laws; and have access to live chat rooms. There are five sites: www.Ex-Lovers.com, www.Ex-Wives.com, www.Ex-Husbands.com, www.Ex-Girlfriends.com and www.Ex-Boyfriends.com

LifeStyles Lover's Revenge

This is a cyber carnival game where you can lob water balloons at human targets. www.lifestyles.com

New Orleans Online Catalog

This is an excellent source for voodoo materials, including special voodoo candles to burn after a break-up. www.noline.com

Revenge Products

This is a wonderful resource for avengers. They sell lots of fun stuff, like a dozen wilting roses, dead mixed floral assortments, funeral wreaths, tombstones, boxes of melted chocolates, black mouth candy, bald man's grooming sets, extra wide toilet paper, small-pecker condoms, *The Gross-Out Cookbook*, and itching powder. www.revengeunlimited.com

Virtual Voodoo Doll by Virtual Design Group.
The user can e-mail an animated voodoo doll complete with sound effects and a personalized message to her mark. www.virtual-design.com

The Voodoo Home Page
This site shows how to use the powers of voodoo to help improve your life. Includes a wide range of books and products for using voodoo in matters of love, evil, and personal power. www.voodoodeprince.com

REVENGE RECIPES

Stinks
Jewellers use a compound called liver of sulphur to turn silver black. This product is available at most serious hobby shops. Activate it with water and it smells awful. It can also be melted together with candle wax and spread on a surface where it will be warmed up, such as on the heating coils of a stove.

Homemade Stink Bombs

Ingredients:

8 ounces ammonia.
Sulphur. Cut off the tips of an entire box of matches or purchase sulphur from a chemist.

Glass bottle, Ziploc bag, or another container that can be both sealed and broken open easily. Ammonium Sulfide smells like rotten eggs, so be sure to seal it tight.

What to do:

1. Place the sulphur or match heads into a bottle or other container.
2. Add the ammonia.
3. Seal the bottle quickly.
4. Shake it up.
5. Open it in a place with little ventilation, like in a parked car or someone's flat.

A down-and-dirty stink bomb can be made with a wooden match and one of those cheap spring-loaded push-button pens.

1. Unscrew the pen shaft, pull out the cartridge, and put it back in reversed so that the open end of the cartridge is sticking out instead of the ballpoint.
2. Put the match in the top of the pen, with the head facing the ballpoint. Screw the pen back together.
3. Pull back the open end of the cartridge (sticking out of the shaft opening) so that the spring tension will fire it into the match head. This will ignite the match inside the pen and create a horrible pungent smell.

Itching Powder
Collect hair clippings from your local hair salon. Mix them with liquid laundry bleach. Let them soak for a couple of hours. Spread the hair out and let it dry, then shred it with scissors or in a blender. Sprinkle it lightly on bedding or in underwear. It makes for ferocious itching, which can only be relieved by showering with lots of heavy-duty soap.

ANONYMOUS REMAILERS

The ability to mail an anonymous letter can be useful in some revenge plots. Contact Anonymous Remailers by mailing them your letter addressed to your mark. Include payment in cash only.

Amy Flynn
P.O. Box R1512
Royal Exchange Post Office
Sydney 2000 Australia
104125@compuserve.com
Charges $6.00 U.S. or Australian
Handles only standard first-class air-mail letters.

Barbara McNeill
14 Verdon St.
Williamstown 3016
Victoria, Australia
Charges $5.00

Dallas Delivers
P.O. Box 64566
Dallas, TX 75206
USA
Charges $1.00

VOODOO SUPPLIES

Books

Urban Voodoo: A Beginner's Guide to Afro-Caribbean Magic. Black, S., Jason and Hyatt, Christopher S. Tempe, Arizona: New Falcon Publications, 1995.

The New Orleans Voodoo Tarot/Book and Card Set.

Martinie, Louis, and Glassman, Sallie Ann. Rochester,
   Vermont: Destiny, 1992.
*The Little Voodoo Kit: Therapy for the Overstressed/Book
   and Voodoo Kit*. Poupette, Jean-Paul. New York: St.
   Martin's Press, 1997.

Stores
Marie Laveau's House of Voodoo
739 Bourbon St.
New Orleans, LA 70116
USA
00 1 (504) 581 3751

Human and animal bone jewellery, funereal artifacts, etc.
Necromance
7220 Melrose Ave.
Los Angeles, CA 90046
USA
00 1 (213) 934 8684

THE AVENGER'S ROLODEX

Skydive Arizona
Annual Junk Day
Skydive Arizona
4900 N. Taylor Road
Eloy, AZ 85231
USA
Tel: 00 1 (520) 466 3753
Fax: 00 1 (520) 466 4720

Beetles, earwigs, cockroaches and other live insects
Many common insects can be found in most pet shops that
sell reptiles (they usually stock live insects as reptile food).

Inland Revenue
To report a tax evader visit your local Inland Revenue office and ask to speak to the special unit of tax investigators known as 'ghostbusters'. Or you can write to:

The Inland Revenue
Somerset House
The Strand
London
WC2

Looped phone numbers in Queensland, Australia
Time Information: 00 61 7 1194
Weather Information: 00 61 7 1196
Boating Conditions: 00 61 7 1190

Rent-a-Kvetch
00 1 (212) 385 2200